Scott Welle
#1 Best Selling Author
Founder, Outperform The Norm

*Dedicated to my brother, Jason, who
motivates and inspires me to
Outperform The Norm.*

DISCLAIMER

This book is not intended as a substitute for the medical advice of physicians. The reader should regularly consult a physician in matters relating to his/her health and particularly with respect to any symptoms that may require diagnosis or medical attention.

Disclaimer and Terms of Use: Effort has been made to ensure that the information in this book is accurate and complete, however, the author and the publisher do not warrant the accuracy of the information, text and graphics contained within the book due to the rapidly changing nature of science, research, known and unknown facts and internet. The Author and the publisher do not hold any responsibility for errors, omissions or contrary interpretation of the subject matter herein. This book is presented solely for motivational and informational purposes only.

I don't believe in "get rich" programs - only in hard work, contributing value and serving others with excellence and consistency. As stipulated by law, I cannot guarantee your ability to get results or earn any money with the information, tools and strategies in this book. Use caution and always consult your accountant, lawyer or professional advisor before acting on this or any information related to a lifestyle change or your business or finances. You alone are the variable and are accountable for the results you get in your life, and by reading this book you agree not to attempt to hold me liable for your decisions, actions or results, at any time, under any circumstance. Sound good?

TABLE OF CONTENTS

- THE -
OUTPERFORMER'S VAULT

A collection of <u>complimentary</u> resources cited in the book to fuel your passion and focus your productivity. This is where Outperform The Norm comes to life. Get them NOW!

Videos:

Audios:

 Total Confidence   Quotes and Life Lessons   Scott's Untold Story

Downloads:

 Performance Analysis   Get Sh%t Done DMO   Training Template

These resources accelerate your progress and take your health, happiness and high performance to the next level. Guaranteed.

Instant Access at:

OutperformTheNorm.com/Vault

INTRODUCTION

I try to live by 5 simple rules in life:

1. Do your best
2. Have fun
3. Treat other people with dignity and respect
4. Stay humble
5. Be true to who you are

I've got the rest of this book to explain to you exactly what I mean by these rules, but let's keep it real from the get-go, shall we?

It took me a year to start writing this book.

Yes, <u>one year</u>. How's THAT for high performance?

When I first conceptualized writing a book, I thought it would be easy. I'd been disciplined enough to write an average of 1-2 blog posts per week for almost a year (60+ total) so I figured I could sit down and crack off a book in 1-2 months, tops.

One year later, I hadn't written a single useable page. I was in a funk. Flat broke and busted. Is it possible to have writer's block for an *entire year*?

Then, finally, I started to look at why it was so difficult for me to get started. And I realized the problem – I was doing a number of things poorly, the most glaringly obvious was trying to write in a style that was not me. I thought that, because I was writing a book, the structure, grammar and tone should be different. I should be big and tough and write the book like my perfectly manicured Master's thesis in graduate school – something that would prove how smart I am, and that would also please the masses. But I never did this when I was writing blog posts (I saw them as more informal) and doing this paralyzed me from writing a single page.

I tell you this because we're living in an age of transparency. With the Internet and social media, you can find out anything about anyone, almost on demand. You can't hide. You are who you say you are.

So, I'll be honest with you – I'm not always healthy. I'm not always happy. And I'm not always high performing. I could stand up tall and puff my chest out and tell you I've got all the answers, but I don't have it all figured out. I'm a very real person (like you) who is just trying to make a difference in this world.

Outperform: *We're not seeking perfection. We're seeking progress.*

However, I do *know* that I have strategies and practical applications that, if you follow them, will dramatically alter the course of your life. It's not magic hocus-pocus – it's grounded principles. Like I always tell my clients – I would never ask you to do something that I have not done myself. It starts with assuming personal accountability for your own life and taking a genuine, honest look at the way you're functioning, contributing, thinking and the decisions you're making, daily. Whether you choose to acknowledge it or not, these decisions are determining your destiny.

Once upon a time I had a client...

"Scott, I REALLY want to make serious changes in my life. I'm fired up! Ready. Motivated!

BUT…I'm really busy right now. My job and life are crazy and I don't have time for ANYTHING…

And they ALWAYS have cookies at the office…

And holidays are coming up…

And it gets dark so early these days…so I don't feel like working out after work…

And it stays dark so late in the morning…so I don't feel like getting out of bed…

And I get hundreds of emails every day…

And I'm soooo addicted to that new reality TV show…

And my dog ate my homework.

So, let me get back to you…SOMEDAY."

I've heard these things before…too many times to count. Let's be clear about one other thing – this book is NOT about someday. This book is about now. Not next month, next week, tomorrow, or even later today. NOW. There are seven days in a week and *Someday* isn't one of them.

Outperform The Norm is a collection of the best strategies used by the healthiest, happiest, highest performing people on the planet. And it's in the palm of your hands. And as you're reading, it's my hope that when you get up from your chair, couch, desk, bed or toilet (or any other location you may be reading), you'll start using the principles in this book immediately. What's the use in waiting?

Outperform: *Successful people don't wait until Someday. Ever.*

Funny, as I'm writing this, I'm on a flight back from San Jose, CA, to Minneapolis, MN (about a 3.5 hour flight). I'm in seat 10C and two people are to my right, two are across the aisle to my left. Of these 4 people, one is watching a movie on his iPad, one is playing a video game, one is sleeping, and one is reading the latest gossip magazine.

I'm writing a book that I hope will change your life.

Don't get me wrong, I have no problem with watching movies, playing video games, reading celebrity gossip or sleeping (obviously – we'll cover its importance later!). The only reason I reference this is because *time* is the single most precious asset we have and we CHOOSE everyday how we will invest it. And if there is something in our lives that we want to accomplish, we'll have to budget the requisite time to make this happen. Anything that wastes time or is incongruent with our desired future has to go. Once time is gone, we never get it back. There are no do-overs.

There's a compound effect to wasted time. It starts innocently enough, where we barely even realize it's happening. But wasted seconds become minutes, minutes become hours, hours become days, days become weeks, weeks become months and months become years. Waste enough seconds and you can waste a good chunk of your life.

I had to learn this lesson the hard way. I've wasted plenty of time and played the blame game with the *Someday Special*. I know you're a busy person. We all are. It's a damn busy world out there. Too much to do in too little time. Most companies lack manpower (or person power?). The average employee is doing the work of 2-3 people...and the only way to get it all done is to work more hours. And sometimes you just want to kick back in row 10 of a long flight, chill out and not have to think.

This is fine...if you're content with who you are, where you're at, where you're going and what you'd like to become. But if you're not satisfied with these things, something needs to change and it will take time to change it. The faster you make changes, the more quickly your desired future comes to fruition and becomes a reality. Wasted time only delays the process. Life isn't a dress rehearsal.

> **Outperform**: *Change doesn't always mean you'll make progress but progress does always mean making a change.*

Back in college, my roommate and I used to sit around and watch movies (usually while recovering from a tough night on the town).

He had a saying after we'd watched a really bad one - he'd look at me and say, *"Ya know, that's 2 hours of my life I'm never going to get back."* He's right. I won't reference which movies prompted this saying, but those unfortunate decisions each took 2 hours from our lives. Over the course of those four college years, I guarantee I wasted not only days, but probably weeks, watching the idiot box. I didn't even notice it was happening.

Outperform: *Our decisions determine our destiny.*

Every decision we make matters. It may not seem like it at the time but it DOES. Consider any of these daily decisions...

- We snooze our alarm for 20-25 minutes or we get out of bed to exercise.

- We get up from our desk to go to the soda machine or we go to the drinking fountain.

- We go out to eat and, for our side, we choose French Fries with the yummy dipping "butt sauce" or we choose steamed broccoli.

- We get stuck in traffic and we stress with road rage or we calmly breathe and let it go.

- We hate our job but stay with the security of a steady paycheck or we risk it all to live with passion and start our own business.

- We plow through our day with blinders and tunnel vision or we stop to ask someone how they're doing when they look sad.

- We check email and social media 20 times a day or we strategically allocate time in the morning and evening to not interrupt our most important tasks.

- We read the morning newspaper (usually filled with negativity, corruption, abuse and scandal) or we quietly prepare for the day by prioritizing and focusing on the positive things we want to accomplish.

- We give up when something looks like it will be too hard or we struggle through it and embrace the process on the way to mastery.

NONE of these singular decisions are bad. Even a few of them won't kill you. But it's the compound effect of doing them over and over and over and over again that shapes the course of your entire life, for better or for worse.

Interestingly, the first three examples will play a key role in your overall health, notably your weight, BMI, body composition, cholesterol, blood pressure, disease, sickness, etc. The second three will affect your happiness, outlook towards life and how much peace you have falling asleep at night. And the last three will affect your performance level, ability to be productive and overall success.

Simple decisions determine your destiny.

It's funny, I run into people all the time who still recognize me from my early days of personal training many years ago. They thought about hiring me then (never did) and some of them contemplate hiring me today (never will). And I hear them singin' the same country-western song: *"I'm just waitin' until xxx and yyy come together, and then things are going to be perfect."*

It'll never happen.

Outperform: *Ready, FIRE, Aim.*

It should NOT be: Ready, aim, aim a little more, and a little more, and a little more...

And omigawd...*SOMEDAY* when I'm in perfect alignment, I'll fire!

A life of perfect alignment isn't something that's given – it's something that's earned. And, sadly, many people never achieve their life of perfect alignment. Something will always be a bit off, keeping them just beneath the Eureka mother-load nirvana of perfection. It doesn't mean they stop fantasizing about it, but this waiting, hoping, for perfect harmony keeps many people from pulling the trigger towards the good things in life. And what many people don't realize is having the courage to pull the trigger and fire is what CREATES a more perfectly aligned life. Not the other way around! Massive action cures all problems.

If you have a life in perfect alignment, where you're 100% fulfilled and content with your levels of health, happiness and high performance, you probably wouldn't be reading this book. And if you are, you're one of the smart, driven few who have made the decisions and utilized the strategies that I will share on the following pages to create a truly amazing life. For that, I commend you. I learn from you and am inspired by you. Let's do lunch.

Here's the Challenge:

The hardest part of doing anything is getting started. It just IS. But momentum is a powerful thing and once something is in motion, it stays in motion (thank you, Sir Issac Newton). This book is about paying attention to and taking action on the small things that have massive results. It is not a miracle, quick fix book. It is not about you, reincarnated as the little engine, sitting around saying "*I think I can, I think I can.*" And it's not about blindly reacting to your days with no idea what will get done or what will be accomplished.

This book contains the unfiltered, straight-up truth about the decisions that will allow you to unlock your greatest potential and to fall asleep at night KNOWING you are making the most of your precious days here on earth. Some parts may be difficult to read. You may not like me (you may not already) but the most difficult things to read are sometimes the things we need to hear the most. They are also the things that produce the greatest results.

I've always had the same mentality since my first day in fitness – I try to move people to action. If you're someone who knows there's something greater out there for you and you're willing to do what it takes to find it, this is the book you've been waiting for.

Let's dig in, Outperformer.

HEALTH

"The state of being free from illness or injury."

THAT is the dictionary definition of health.

Really? Aren't we setting the bar kind of low?

Minnesota has a notoriously huge state fair every August. Basic premise of the fair: take any food, bread it, deep fry it, put it on a stick and, if possible, coat it in sugar or chocolate. Heart valve blockage and artery clogging comes included.

I LOVE Minnesotans but I know many of these people I see at the state fair are not "ill" (per se) and not injured, yet I would still not consider them "healthy."

First, Outperforming health is not a state. Similar to happiness, it is an ongoing condition you *create* by your daily lifestyle choices. Plain and simple.

Do you have the energy, stamina, vitality, endurance and strength to do what you want to do, when you want to do it, on command? If you don't, there's only one person to blame (the mirror knows the answer).

Thankfully, this book will help.

Despite the dictionary, true health can still be a difficult concept to define. When you're there, you know it. When you're not there, you forget what it feels like (assuming you've been there before). It's a vicious cycle – healthy behaviors trigger more healthy behaviors. Unhealthy behaviors trigger more unhealthy behaviors. Yes, exercise triggers more exercise and ice cream triggers more ice cream. And, even if it's not necessarily what's *best* for our body, the hardest thing is to turn it around when our behaviors are going in the wrong direction. We'd rather continue on, uninterrupted, regardless of the consequences.

My brother and I have made it a tradition to run at least one marathon together each year. We plod along shoulder-to-shoulder, soaking up the race-day atmosphere and laughing the whole way (or for the first 18-20 miles, at least). It's a blast. Brotherly bonding at its finest.

A few years ago we ran the Memphis marathon. I know from my background in bioenergetics that I will burn anywhere from 2500-3000 calories running a marathon, depending on my fitness level, the temperature and how fast we run it. Like always, the race was a ton of fun, and the nice thing about completing a marathon is that you've obviously got some "wiggle room" in terms of what you can eat and drink. Your metabolism is stoked.

So, we had a few donuts and cookies immediately post-race. No big deal – we eat like that after *every* marathon we run. Then we drove 3+ hours south to Greenwood, MS, where my brother was living. Greenwood is a small town in the heart of the Mississippi valley and is mostly "free from illness or injury." And because of my brother's involvement in the church, we were invited to parties and social functions *every* day and *every* night.

Every one of them included food...and I'm not talking salads and vegetables. These meals were more "substantial."

The next three days were a blur of brutally unhealthy, deep-fried and fat laden foods (I vaguely remember having duck wrapped in bacon?), usually combined with lemonade and/or sweet tea. I actually think drinking water was illegal. By the time I boarded my flight back to MN on Wednesday night (race was on Sunday), I've never felt *worse* in my life.

I was wickedly hung over...from FOOD.

It's funny how you can do something healthy like run a marathon and feel like you're at the pinnacle of health and fitness, yet in the span of three days; totally turn it around by your own lifestyle choices. It took me *days* after I got home to get back into a healthy "routine." Because I felt so badly, I didn't want to eat well. I didn't want to work out. I didn't even want to get off the couch.

Outperform: *How you look and feel are direct results of how you CHOOSE to live your life.*

One thing is certain – the human body is PHENOMENALLY adaptive. Consider the alcoholic who can drink a bottle of vodka and still maintain mental function. Consider the smoker who can burn through two packs a day and still have functional lung capacity. And consider the Ironman triathlete who can condition the body to withstand the rigors of a 140.6-mile competition and still be physically active afterwards.

Each of these conditions signifies an adaptation. We are what we repeatedly do. And the problem with defining "healthy," is that many people, if they're in a process of negative adaptation, cannot even remember what _true_ health feels like. They may be reading this book while eating duck wrapped in bacon with a sweet tea chaser. More power to them. And if they're functioning just fine in their day-to-day existence and are free from illness or injury, they must be "healthy." Right?

Wrong.

If health was wealth, that's like saying everyone who is not on welfare is rich. We need higher standards of excellence.

The Gap

The Gap is the discrepancy between what we know and what we actually do. Studies have shown that 90% of people who have had major heart surgery will no longer be correctly taking their life-saving medication after six months. If it were all about doing what we're "supposed to do," we wouldn't be having this conversation. This book wouldn't be necessary and wellness wouldn't be a trillion dollar industry.

> **Outperform:** *If something is good for you, DO IT. This isn't rocket science.*

Enter the words of the late Steve Jobs, *"People don't know what they want until you show it to them."* Most people have *no idea* how good they can feel if they would just make a few SIMPLE changes.

That's where I'll leave the definition of health. I assume if you're reading this right now you're either a) in good health already, or b) believe that there is something better for you on the other side.

But because your body will, literally, adapt to anything you're doing (drugs, exercise, nutrition, sleep, stress, etc.), MOST people will never open their eyes to the fact that there is the possibility for Outperforming health and what it can do for them. They adopt the "if it ain't broke, don't fix it," mentality. But even if it ain't "broke" (in the traditional sense), can't we still work to build it BETTER?

This is what I want for you – I want you to feel what it's like to be alive in your own skin. Yes, *alive!* Like, if a bear were to jump out of the woods you could quickly move away from it. I want you to have that mouth-watering dessert and know that you've created a roaring metabolism that will easily burn it off. I want you to have the energy to accomplish everything you want to accomplish during the day and sleep soundly at night. And I want your body to be resistant to fatigue and illness so you can enjoy quality time with the people who are important to you and appreciate the finer things that life has to offer.

THAT is Outperforming health.

NUTRITION

Feed The Machine

You are what you eat. Literally.

Your body is *constantly* rebuilding itself. It never stops. Your stomach lining will be replaced in three days. Your skin will be replaced in two weeks. Your liver will be replaced in one year. Your entire human skeleton will be replaced within 8-10 years.

This is why most people can feel so amazing in such a short period of time (and vice versa). Your body is, literally, not even the same as it once was...all the way down to the cellular level.

You get to choose whether you build this body out of processed junk or quality whole foods.

Outperform: *What you shove into your mouth becomes you.*

First, appreciate that your body is wonderfully complex. Sophisticated machines are built after it. Its ability to repair, rebuild, recover, adapt and fight off infection is unparalleled. Sometimes we lose sight of this.

When I was growing up, our family would take a 2-day "vacation" every year to stay at the Holiday Inn in St. Cloud, Minnesota. I loved it. My brother and I each got to bring a friend and we were each given a roll of quarters to spend in the arcade room.

Our favorite game? Ms. Pacman, which is, quite possibly, the best arcade game ever made (my brother would say the same). We'd have contests to see who could get the top score. And for every quarter you got three "lives." After you lost the three lives, the machine would start counting down "15...14...13...12...11..." and you had the option to insert another quarter before time ran out if you wanted to keep going.

We'd all be screaming, *"FEED THE MACHINE! FEED THE MACHINE!"*

You give the machine what it needs; you get to keep going. You don't give it what it needs - game over.

Outperform: *Your body is a machine. Feed it what it needs if you want it to keep going.*

From now on, food is not food. Food is fuel. Food is energy. Food is the quarter that allows you to continue playing. All athletes and Outperformers understand this. You put a certain amount of fuel into your body; you will get a certain amount of production out of it.

My girlfriend loves to give me grief about this. I've created and conditioned my metabolism to where, if I don't eat roughly every 2-3 hours, it is *very* difficult for me to function. I've worked with a lot of corporate executives who can be highly functional the whole day without food. I'm NOT that person. My machine needs fuel or it's game over.

Again, this speaks to the wonder of the human body. It will ALWAYS adapt to what it is you're doing. Even if you're not giving it the fuel it needs, it will find a way to create energy to keep you going. And, whether you realize it or not, when you starve your body it will usually create energy by eating into your lean muscle tissue (the very thing that most people want more of). It's a starvation survival mechanism that kicks in, regardless of your current health and fitness level.

This chapter is about your peak health and it's your choice whether you want to listen. Even if you eat garbage, or don't eat anything at all, your body will find a way to function. It always adapts and it will compensate by whatever means necessary to make it work. But I'm telling you there's a *better* way and it's a lot simpler than most people appreciate.

Here are my top six strategies for feeding a well-oiled, efficient, durable, highly productive machine:

1. Breakfast

Feeding the machine starts with breakfast. My mother was correct when she told me it's the most important meal of the day. Every day when you wake up you're starting from a standstill and you choose which direction you're going to go. Solid breakfast starts you in the direction of a healthy, productive day. A poor breakfast (or skipping it altogether) starts you in the direction of an unhealthy, low energy day.

Think about it – you don't drive your car on an empty tank of gas, so why do you try to drive your body with an empty tank? Do you *really* believe it's going to perform as well when it's running on vapor? Putting fuel into your body within one hour of waking up will kick start your metabolism and set the tone for your entire day.

The word *Breakfast* comes from "breaking-a-fast." That's what you're doing. You've been fasting since you had your last meal the day before which, assuming you've slept roughly 6-8 hours (what most Americans do), means you're probably looking at breaking a 10-12 hour fast by the time you finally have breakfast.

I've been to enough Monday morning meetings, seminars, networking events and presentations to know what the typical breakfast looks like for working Americans. It's what I refer to as the "high carb breakfast." Donuts, bagels, muffins, pastries, breads, fruits and juices all cause our blood sugar to immediately spike, only to plummet roughly an hour later, where the coffee pot better be close by or we're in big trouble.

The reason this is the usual breakfast – it is easy, convenient, fairly non-perishable and cheap. All that would be required to stabilize blood sugar would be to add protein, but protein is harder to prepare, more perishable and more expensive. Why bother? Even if we're head bobbing until the coffee kicks in, we'll get through it.

Another thing I hear from clients constantly, *"but, Scott, my cravings are so bad at night!"* Most people don't realize that there is a direct link between being under-caloried (not eating enough) early in the day and being over-caloried (eating too much) later on. Your body always WANTS and NEEDS fuel...and it will do its best to compensate if you've been running on empty all day.

Outperform: *Eat more early and you'll eat less late.*

This book is about your daily decisions. Regardless of your current level of health, happiness and high performance, each day when you wake up is a fresh new opportunity to make the most of your day. What you do for breakfast paves the way for everything after it. If you have a crap-filled breakfast of carbs, fats and sugars, do you *really* think you're going to make healthy choices for lunch and dinner? Heck no. *Nobody* does this...not even me. You've already got the ball rolling down unhealthy hill and it takes a lot more effort to stop it and turn it around in the other direction than if you would have just rolled it in the right direction to begin with.

Choose breakfast wisely. It will make or break your day.

2. Timing of Fuel

Feed the machine every 2-3 hours. Your car has a super small gas tank and it needs to be filled constantly. If you don't, you'll be back on empty. This keeps your energy levels up, your metabolism stoked, your insulin levels stable and your mental clarity focused (your brain consumes 25% of the body's nutrients for energy).

This is one of the most difficult things for people. Our typical lifestyles are not conducive to fueling our bodies this way. We're built for 3 square meals a day of breakfast, lunch and dinner.

Typical day for most people:

- Skip breakfast (snoozed alarm too many times. In a rush to get out the door)
- Average lunch
- Big dinner

Slightly better day:

- "High carb" breakfast
- Average lunch
- Big dinner

Ideal day:

- Balanced breakfast
- Mid-morning snack
- Average lunch
- Mid-afternoon snack
- Average dinner

Timing of fueling is critically important. Small portion sizes, frequently.

Energy drink companies have built their entire campaigns (you know which ones I'm talking about) on what you're going to feel like at 2pm. Why? Because they know the daily choices most people make. They know people usually skip breakfast (and even fewer will have mid morning snacks), so when they get to lunch, they'll overeat to compensate for lack of fuel in the morning. They'll also have the wrong combinations (discussed next). Because of this, the average person can barely get through the afternoon without some type of artificially enhanced energy.

Outperform: *You know that 2pm feeling? It's called EAT A BETTER LUNCH.*

Portions sizes in our country have gotten out of control. Plates are bigger than ever and we're almost always looking for the most bang for our buck out of food (which means as much as possible for as cheap as possible). The interesting thing I've found in working with people over the years is that, when you focus on eating every 2-3 hours, portion sizes take care of themselves.

I'm a prime example. I was always playing sports growing up, so by the time I would get home at night after practice or a game, I was *starved*. My mom would cook something and I would load up my plate as full as it would possibly go. And I would shovel it in as fast as I could because I was always told I couldn't leave the dining room table until I was finished.

Interesting introduction to food, huh?

What this taught me was to ignore the basic signs of *satiety*, or what it feels like to be full, and actually STOP eating then. I thought that you ate until what was in front of you was gone. I didn't know any other way. I once famously ate 14 tacos from Taco Bell while at a basketball tournament in Fargo, ND. I'm still the guy who can clean everyone else's plate when we're out for dinner. You put it in front of me; it's getting done.

So, in college when I started geeking out over health and high performance, I had to CONDITION my body (I emphasize the word *condition*) to eat more often, with smaller portion sizes. I still find that if I'm not cognizant of eating every 2-3 hours, I will gravitate towards eating the way I grew up.

3. Type of Fuel

Feed your machine with the correct *type* of fuel. Lots of protein, complex carbs, vegetables, healthy fats and fruits. Do this and your car will run efficiently. Don't do this and your car will be shaking and spitting out green exhaust.

There are some general rules of thumb when choosing what to feed your machine:

I) The less processed, the better.

How processed something is deals with the number of times the food has been altered before it enters your mouth. Candy and licorice have been altered much more than broccoli and cauliflower.

When foods are processed, they are stripped of most of their vital nutrients. Vital nutrients are what make foods perishable. Foods are not meant to last weeks and months – they are meant to be consumed. I recently saw a video on someone who had saved a McDonald's hamburger for <u>14 years</u> and it had not spoiled. Think about the number of vital nutrients you are getting the next time you go through the drive thru.

Outperform: *If your fridge is full of spoiling foods, good job. You've got the right fuel.*

Our country is malnourished. Not in the traditional sense, where we think of starving children in third world countries begging for food. The evolution of our agribusiness has created a unique society that can be overfed, yet still undernourished.

You can have 10,000 calories a day of pizza, but if it's not satisfying your basic nutritional deficiencies, it doesn't matter. You're malnourished. You're not going to feel the way you want to feel. You won't be healthy. You're not feeding your machine. Better to let that food go to waste...before it goes to waist.

This is a huge problem for calorie-counters. It's often not about the calories – it's about the *type* of calories that matters. You can have 2,000 calories of brussel sprouts or 2,000 calories of French fries and, even though it's equal in terms of calorie counting, it will function vastly different in your body (and look vastly different on your body as well).

"Skinny fat" is a very real problem as well, related to above. Skinny fat is what happens when someone is normal weight (or even underweight), yet is still malnourished. Usually this happens because the person doesn't eat...or they have the wrong fuel. They have a large amount of visceral fat (fat protecting their organs), are usually prone to infection and are almost always very tired as well. They've got the double whammy of being under-caloried and under-nourished.

Outperform: *Feed your machine nutrients, not calories.*

II) The less sodium, the better.

Sodium typically goes hand in hand when food is being processed. The average person should not have more than 2,000mg of sodium throughout the day, and if you're not careful, you can easily have that in one meal. Sodium causes dehydration and high blood pressure. And most people who seek to lose weight have no idea how much water they're retaining because of excess sodium.

III) The fewer ingredients, the better.

Less is more. Less than 10 ingredients is good. Less than 5 ingredients is great. If you cannot pronounce the ingredients, you're in trouble. Everybody can pronounce "kale."

Another simple way to look at this is if it comes in a bag, box, pouch or package, be careful. Usually this means it is processed, has more sodium, has more ingredients, and is a generally unhealthy fuel. I've never had someone ask me if broccoli is healthy.

Outperform: *If you have to ask whether something is healthy, save your breath. It isn't.*

On the following pages are lists of the foods that you need to feed your machine. Eat these MOST of the time and you'll look, feel and perform at your maximum. **Also see the

Outperformer's Vault for a downloadable comprehensive list of these fuels.

Outperformer's Lean Protein

Egg Whites
Turkey (not from Deli)
Lean Ground Turkey Breast
Salmon
Halibut
Orange Roughy
Swordfish
Tuna
Shrimp
Chicken Breasts (Boneless/Skinless)
Buffalo/Bison
Greek Yogurt
Cottage Cheese
Tofu
Black Beans
Nut Butter
Soy/Almond Milk

Protein is the basic building block of muscle and is one of the most difficult things to get enough of, especially when you're on the go. If you can't make the above choices, look for a quality bar or meal replacement shake with a 1:1 ratio of carbs: protein.

Outperformer's
Complex Carbohydrates

Wild Rice
Brown Rice
Sweet Potatoes
Barley
Lentils
Steel Cut Oats
Cream of Wheat
Whole Grain Oatmeal
Muesli
Tortillas (whole grain)
Pitas (whole grain)
Couscous
Quinoa
Beans
Bagels (whole grain or *"Everything"*)
Whole Grain Pasta

Your body needs carbohydrates (the right kind) to function. Have them liberally and always with protein.

Outperformer's Healthy Fats

Canola Oil
Extra Virgin Olive Oil
Flaxseed Oil
Nut Butter (also mentioned in protein)
Pecans
Walnuts
Almonds
Pine Nuts
Water Chestnuts
Pistachios
Avocados

Healthy fats are good for the body. Don't go nuts (literally and figuratively) on these items, as fats are still higher in overall calories, but definitely include them in your daily nutrition.

Outperformer's
Fresh Fruit

Bananas
Apples
Cantalope
Grapes
Grapefruit
Peaches
Strawberries
Blueberries
Raspberries
Blackberries
Pomegranates
Lemon
Lime
Cherries
Pears
Pineapples

The "ripeness" of a fruit slightly changes its glycemic index, or sugar content. Choose less ripe fruits for a more stable blood sugar response.

Outperformer's Fibrous Vegetables

Broccoli
Zucchini
Kale
Tomatoes
Bell Peppers
Asparagus
Carrots
Spinach
Celery
Cucumber
Radishes
Mushrooms
Cauliflower
Onions
Green Beans
Alfalfa Sprouts
Brussel Sprouts
Cabbage

Fresh is best. Steamed is second. Boiled is third. Sauteed is last.

4. Hydration

We live in a chronically dehydrated society. Soda, energy drinks, coffee, tea and sodium leave us in a never-ending state of catch up in hydration. Our daily routine creates a general imbalance between products that suck water out and those that put water back in.

Consider:

- A healthy body is made up of 60-70% water
- Muscles are made up of about 80% water
- As little as a 1-2% difference in dehydration can affect performance, cognitive function and decision making

Water is necessary and essential for peak health. Embrace it or live at The Norm.

We've all heard that we should drink eight 8-ounce glasses of water each day. I've got a slightly different formula – I advocate we drink a minimum of half our body weight in ounces of water, daily. So, if you weigh 128 pounds, eight 8-ounce glasses is a good starting point. If you weigh 150 pounds you should target 75 ounces, and if you weigh 200 pounds you should target 100 ounces.

$$Water\ (ounces) = \frac{Bodyweight\ (pounds)}{2}$$

Seems manageable, right?

But there's a catch. Soda, energy drinks, coffee, tea and alcohol all have negative impacts on our hydration. They are diuretics (pull water out). Thus, if we wish to stay hydrated we need to drink even *more* water than recommended above.

Understanding why you need to drink more water is fairly simple...

Your heart pumps blood. Blood contains hemoglobin. Hemoglobin contains oxygen. Muscles need oxygen to function. The faster the muscles get oxygen, the better they perform. Hydrated blood gets to muscles faster.

The same exact thing happens with the brain via the Central Nervous System. It needs oxygen to function, which is why hydration key to mental alertness, decision-making and overall cognitive performance.

> **Outperform:** *The single BEST thing you can do for your brain, and body, is to drink water.*

If you're still not convinced, here are the other

benefits of water:

- Improved mental clarity
- Increased metabolism
- Better skin
- Controlled hunger cravings
- Improved digestion and absorption of nutrients
- Less back and joint pain
- Reduced risk of cancer
- Improved flexibility
- More energy
- Detoxifies the body

5. Your Feeding "Relationship"

Americans have very unhealthy relationships with food. There's no need to sugarcoat it – it's the truth. Studies have shown we spend more time thinking about whether a food is healthy, yet we're the unhealthiest country on the planet. Try to figure that one out? If you're thinking about something, shouldn't it be easier to make it happen?

Outperform: *Our abusive relationship with food is killing us.*

I had a former client with a very troubled food relationship. Endurance sports tend to attract a more obsessive-compulsive personality to begin with, but this person was the extreme of the extremes. Sometimes it was difficult to watch. It was one or the other, all or none, black or white, with no shades of grey.

Because of this, she could not have a few bites of dessert. It was either no dessert or give her the whole thing. No candy or the full bag. No drinks or the whole bottle of wine. The word "moderation" was not in her vocabulary.

It's beyond the scope of my expertise to be able to *cure* a severely abusive relationship with food but I recognized a lack of balance that was not only psychologically draining, but physically and emotionally draining as well. On one hand, it requires a lot of energy to completely *resist* something. Think about when you were younger and your parents told you that you couldn't have something – you wanted it *that* much more, right? Food is no different. Tell yourself that you can't have something and you'll waste more energy wanting it.

It's also a huge energy expenditure to feel guilty over eating or drinking much more than you know you should. You restrict...and restrict...and restrict...and restrict...and, finally, you GIVE IN. It happens to everyone *eventually*. And when you finally do, it feels great at the time, but afterwards you're consumed because you know you shouldn't have done it. This becomes a vicious cycle and is very much a binge-purge mentality.

Weird as it sounds, you need to create a "relationship" with food. Yes, a RELATIONSHIP...one in which you are entering into it with your eyes wide open. You are asking food to help you with something (give you energy, make you more productive). It has to meet you in the middle and deliver these results.

Unfortunately, we use food to deliver a different result much of the time. Much like an abusive relationship with a partner, we abuse food. We use it as a punching bag to absorb our own emotional garbage. We have a stressful day; we eat. We feel depressed; we eat. We feel angry; we eat. We feel great; we eat. And, in a lot of these cases, we eat the *same* thing. It usually isn't broccoli and celery sticks.

Outperform: *It's not what you do SOME of the time; it's what you do MOST of the time that matters.*

The Rule of 90 Percent

An all or nothing mentality can be one of the biggest detractors to progress in any area of your life – exercise, nutrition, business, or anything else. Because we often think we have to "be 100% committed to eating healthy" or it doesn't really matter, right? We have to perpetually resist the temptation to have dessert or it doesn't even pay to be "dieting," right?

Do you know that more than 60% of people who join a health club will quit after six months? Do you know that more than 75% of people who "diet" will gain all the weight back they lost, and then some?

Why is this?

Here's the truth – people quit health clubs and fail at diets because they aren't able to find balance between being on an exercise program and eating healthy, and doing nothing at all. They miss one day of exercise and they become a little less motivated...then it happens again...and again...before you know it, they've quit. So it goes for dieting as well.

The answer – follow the rule of 90%.

If you can do anything well 90% of the time you're going to be very successful. I use this in almost all areas of my life...and most of my clients do as well.

Working Out & Training: hitting 90% of my workouts for a given week is a great week. Notice I didn't even say a "good" week...I said

GREAT week. I almost never hit all the workouts I have planned because life happens and sometimes things come up. But I never beat myself up when they do. Even my most committed clients never hit every workout, every week, every month. That's ok. When I say, "hit," I simply mean doing the entire workout at the proper intensities and durations. Sometimes things get cut short.

Nutrition: eat well 90% of the time. When I'm able to do this I feel good and I never feel guilty. But eating well 90% of the time means that you're eating WELL 90% of the time (not "kinda well"). Eating well most of the time means I never feel bad about having full-fat ice cream and heavy, dark beer the other 10% of the time. I've earned it.

Business & Personal: I usually start every day with a list of things I want to accomplish (on notecards, see High Performance chapter). I also have a slightly broader list that defines the goals for the week. If I cross 90% of the items off those lists by the end of the week I know I've made *significant* progress. Then I can watch TV or a movie…or generally do something "relaxing"…and not worry about the other stuff that should be getting done.

Your relationship with food is no different than a relationship with a significant other – there must be times of compromise. If you really enjoy desserts and it's difficult for you to resist them, what kind of compromise can you come to that will make that relationship work? Relationships aren't always peachy and perfect – they require WORK. But if you're able to focus on the positive accomplishment of the 90% instead of the negative derailment of the 10%, you're going to make massive changes in all areas of your life.

Are you listening to me??? I'm being serious here!

In general, there are two types of people:

1 – The "One time and I'm good"

These people function well by knowing there is *one day* of the week that they are able to have their vice food (in this case, dessert). If this sounds like you, would this be a legitimate compromise in your pursuit of health? It would be a great start...if you can stick to it. But if one day often becomes two or three days, you're not this type of person and you may want to revise this line of thinking.

One caveat if you're the *one time and I'm good* type of person – eat your food and feel damn good about it. Don't think about whether it's healthy or whether you *should* be doing it – just eat it. Love it. Savor it. Now's not the time to choose portion control or fat free. Have whatever you want to and feel good about it because you've *earned* it. Beating yourself up over it is only going to drain your mental and emotional energy.

You may hear a lot of people refer to this as the "cheat day." That's fine – call it what you want to. I'm taking the relationship analogy a little bit too far if I start talking about you cheating on food.

2 – The "Just gimme a little bit"

These people need to "wet their whistle" more often than one time a week. But, when they do, they don't need nearly as much of something. In the end, if we're talking about desserts, they end up consuming roughly the same amount as the *one time and I'm good's* do. A bite or two most of the days usually equates to having the whole thing once a week.

An ex-girlfriend of mine had more self-restraint than anyone I've ever met. Her eating habits drove me nuts (in a good way) because they were the exact opposite of mine. We'd go out to dinner and both order desserts. She'd eat one or two bites of hers and give the rest to me. I'd rip down my whole dessert AND what was left of hers. Again, you put it in front of me; it's getting done. And I always respected her for being able to have her one or two bites and be done with it. This just wasn't my personality.

If you are wired where you just need the little taste but you don't need the whole thing, have some of these foods, often. A little bit every day or every other day isn't going to kill you. It may even be better than taking down half the cake one time per week.

Link to the End Result

If you continuously eat things that you know you shouldn't, all you need to do is think of the END RESULT of eating a food. What are you asking food to give you? Are you eating *because* you feel a certain way? Or eating because you want food to make you *feel* a certain way? Or both?

Studies have shown that a key characteristic to being an Outperformer is delaying gratification. This means that, as much as you may want to eat something in the moment, you're able to link the negative feelings or repercussions from certain behaviors and put off their momentary desire. You see the end game.

So, the next time you're looking at a burger and fries, think about how you'll feel 2 hours later. Or if you want a piece of cake, how will you feel the next time you look in the mirror. Or if you want a few glasses of wine, how you'll feel the next morning.

A key to any behavior change, nutrition or otherwise, is seeing the eventual result that will come from it. Outperformers do not respond to urges and cravings.

Eating Out of Boredom

Many people simply eat out of boredom. If they're watching TV, they eat. If they're on the computer, they eat. If they're alone at home, they eat.

These things are not about urges and cravings as much as they're about habitual behavior. If you want to change a behavior, interrupt your pattern. Do something else to stay occupied while you're watching TV, sitting at the computer or home alone. If you keep yourself occupied with something else that you would normally fill with eating, you'll find that you don't even miss it.

6. Planning

Hundreds of years ago our ancestors were uncertain of where their next meal was coming from and they would venture out into the wilderness in search of food. They couldn't come home until they were able to provide for their family. When they found food, they came home. If they couldn't find food, they continued searching.

You're not them. Plan your meals.

Outperform: *Failing to plan is planning to fail.*

When you wake up in the morning you should have a good idea *exactly* what you're going to eat, when. Your meals are planned...just like you would plan any other meetings, events, reminders, etc. They're a high priority task in your schedule.

Back to the car analogy – not planning your meals is like driving your car near empty and continuing to drive until a gas station magically pops up. You may already be running on vapor or you may have a little fuel left, but it's variable and inconsistent at best. Wouldn't it be a lot less stressful and better for you in the long term to plan when you're going to stop at the gas station?

Planning only takes 5-10 minute per day, max. Assuming you've done the proper grocery shopping, you've already got the right foods. Simply look at your schedule (almost everyone has it in their calendar on their phone) and look at your food. Then ask yourself, "*What will I eat, when?*"

For *what* you're going to eat, refer to the Type of Fuel chapter. For *when* you're going to eat it, refer to the Timing of Fuel chapter. Why do we make this so hard?

I can hear you saying, "But, Scott, you don't understand how busy I am." Yes, I do. Everyone is busy. The same way a corporate executive is running from meeting to meeting, a stay-at-home mom is running from drop off to pick up. But we all have 5-10 minute gaps and, as long as you've planned, that's all it takes.

The fact is, most people let their day plan their meals instead of their meals plan their day. If they would take a few minutes the night before (or the morning of) and THINK about when they realistically have a gap in their schedule to be able to eat, it would be a game changer. It only takes this initial acclimation process too. Once you have conditioned your body to eat throughout the course of the day, it will start TELLING you when it needs food, instead of allowing you to plow through the entire day running your car on empty.

For most people, you're only really talking about planning two meals: mid-morning snack and mid-afternoon snack. TWO! Breakfast will be eaten before you leave the house, most people have lunch already (either make a healthy selection when you go out or bring a meal with you) and dinner is either at home or at a restaurant.

No one is so busy that they cannot have something in the middle of the morning and something in the middle of the afternoon. If convenience is an absolute necessity, choose a good meal replacement bar or shake. I normally refer to these as "fake foods" because you cannot live off them (actually, you could, but whole foods should still be the staple of your fueling), but they do make a good nutritional choice for people on the run.

Shape The Environment

Shape the environment is a simple term I use for clients – it means to make success as easy as possible. Why in heck wouldn't you want to do that?

Example – you know you need to drink more water. Do you really want to have to get up and go to the drinking fountain every time you need to drink? Or do you want to have to pull into the convenience store to buy a new bottle of water every time you're empty?

Wouldn't it be easier to have a big bottle of water with you at your desk? Or wouldn't it make more sense to have a case of water sitting in your car that you could access at any time?

Outperform: *Make success as easy as possible on yourself.*

You'd be surprised at how few people take the time to make success easy. They decide they're going to start a morning exercise routine but don't have a clue what they're going to wear in the morning, what they need to bring to the gym, what they'll eat when they're done and what they'll wear afterwards. So, when their alarm goes off, the first thoughts that pop into their head are all things they need to do *other* than the main purpose of going to the gym in the first place (to exercise!).

Contrast this with the successful person who has shaped their environment and made it easy. They've set out their workout clothes the night before, put a water bottle and a protein bar in their workout bag and organized their clothes that they'll need to wear to work afterwards. When their alarm goes off in the morning, all they need to do is get up, grab their items and get out the door. And this planning probably took less than 5 minutes.

Anytime you're going to try to change a behavior or do something differently, the

FIRST thing you should ask yourself is what you can do to make this change as easy as possible. Make it easy and it'll likely happen. Make it hard and your chances of success go down dramatically.

Examples of Shaping the Environment:

Nutrition: cooking meals and putting them in Tupperware to eat during the weak. I normally cook meals on Sunday and Wednesday nights...and I cook enough to have 3 days worth of meals.

Hydration: always have a water bottle with you and have a case of water in your car.

Business: delegating the tasks that you shouldn't be doing. If you're not good at something, outsource it. If it takes you longer than it would take someone else, outsource it. Don't waste time trying to "figure it out" if it's not crucial to the results of the business.

Personal: only check social media and email at set times during the day. Most people waste hours per day doing this when the time could be invested in relationships, personal development, hobbies or tasks and errands.

Case Study of a Personal Trainer

When I first started as a personal trainer, my job was, basically, to kick someone's ass (in a good, safe way) for the hour and then let them go on their way. Maybe we discussed some of what they were doing outside of the club during the session but usually they were breathing too heavy by mid-session to talk to me much about what they were doing.

Sounds like fun, huh?

Even by doing this, most of my clients saw great results. But there were still a percentage of them that didn't. This bothered me because I couldn't figure out *why* it was happening. I'd ping pong between "my clients are uncommitted weaklings," and "I'm a horrible trainer." In actuality, neither of these was correct.

I simply wasn't focusing enough on the big picture and helping clients adopt the proper fueling habits in their daily lives, which is the basic nature of the personal training industry. Most of the focus is on the 1-3 hours when the person is in the gym, in front of you. What about the other 165-167 hours? Aren't they more important?

Yes, they are.

What I came to realize: I could beat someone up until they were blue in the face for 1-3 hours a week but these hours alone were never going to get the person the results that they wanted. This is part of the reason that there has been a huge boom in health coaching and life coaching. People NEED help on shaping the environment and balancing some of these things in their daily lives.

The Positivity of Permission

We live in a society of negativity. Sorry, it's true. It starts with the media, which often focuses more on negative greed, corruption, scandal and what's *wrong*, rather than what's positive and what's *right*.

Looking at food should be no different.

I'm betting almost every single person reading this book has tried a "diet" at *some* point in life. And the first thought that is triggered when someone decides to go on a diet is what they need to *cut out*...or what they need to *restrict*. Correct me if I'm wrong, but isn't this a negative mindset?

It sets you up for failure. When someone tells you that you can't have something, what's the first thing you think about?

Exactly.

Outperform: *What do the first three letters of "DIET" spell? Enough said.*

When I was younger I used to love "Freezies" (they were basically flavored popsicles) in the summer when it was hot outside. But many times when I'd been bad (oh yeah, it happened often) my mother would tell me I couldn't have any Freezies.

And when she would tell me that, all I'd think about for the rest of the day was how much I wanted a Freezie. It was hell. I was like Pavlov's dog sitting there, salivating.

Most of us have an experience like this from when we were younger. We were bad and something was taken away from us as punishment. And usually, what was taken away from us was something we really liked.

Can you see how this relates to food?

Whenever people think about making changes in their nutritional strategy, they start thinking about depriving themselves of the things they really enjoy. This, in turn, makes them want it even more. From this point forward, their "diet" is nothing more than a battle of willpower of their mind vs. food. The power of the human mind is incredible but food almost always wins this fight.

But this time, there's no mother holding you accountable, telling you that you can't have something. It's up to YOU to hold yourself accountable. If you're lucky, you've enlisted the help of a coach, friend or spouse to hold you accountable...but even this person can often not be with you 24/7.

It's time to change your attitude towards the positivity of permission (POP), or one of empowerment.

Outperform: *You will never win a war with food. Raise the white flag and surrender now.*

A while back I worked with a sales manager with an IT (Informational Technology) software company. He was one of my first "official" clients where I was going to enhance his overall life performance by improving his nutrition, hydration, supplementation, exercise, stress and recovery. No stone was going to be left unturned.

This guy was a HIGH performer. Extremely driven, Type-A, hard working and would do whatever it took to get the job done. He had a very disciplined, "militaristic" personality. And what made it even more phenomenal was the fact that he was running his body on empty day after day after day. He had maximized his ability to run on vapor.

His fueling strategy:

Breakfast: coffee x 3 (possibly a bagel if they had them at the office)

Mid-morning: coffee x 2

Lunch: burger or sandwich + fries

Mid-afternoon: coffee x 2

Dinner: whatever the wife was making (pizza, steak, tacos – very inconsistent)

Yes, you're reading this correctly. He was drinking 7-8 cups of coffee a day and NO water – he was operating the entire day on very little food. His blood must have been thick like motor oil from dehydration. But, again, the human body is amazing and will find a way to function when it needs to. In his case, it only functioned because it was so artificially amped up on caffeinated coffee that it had no choice.

Sadly, I came to realize this is more typical than I once thought. I won't deal with the other aspects of his life, but to focus on the POP, instead of the NOR (*Negativity of Restriction*), the first thing I had him do was add in water (I was worried if I asked him to cut down on his coffee that he would get violent with me!).

Adding in water will make you feel more alert and energized strictly from a hydration standpoint, which will, in turn, cut down on the reliance on coffee.

Next up on the POP was to add in morning fuel, or breakfast. I wasn't going to sweat the bagel but to stabilize blood sugar levels; he needed to add in some protein to that. Similar to adding in water, this would give him more consistent energy throughout the morning and less peaks and valleys.

Third on the POP is to add in fruit to lunch. He agreed to do this instead of French fries so we can technically claim this as a substitution, but fruit will further bolster his hydration for the afternoon. And truthfully, I'm most concerned about the coffee in the mid-afternoon anyway. Doing this significantly impacts your stress and cortisol levels, and your ability to sleep.

Fourth on the POP was to add in complex carbohydrates and vegetables to dinner. Since his wife was already doing the majority of the cooking, I told him to "politely request" (I cannot be held responsible for domestic disturbances) that she add in these things. Most of the meals she was cooking already included protein and this request doesn't require any more effort – it just gives the meal a more strategic focus. Of course she obliged.

His "after" fueling strategy:

Breakfast: coffee x 3, 20 oz. of water, bagel with turkey bacon

Mid-morning: coffee x 2, 8 oz. of water

Lunch: burger or sandwich + fruit, 20 oz. of water

Mid-afternoon: coffee x 2, 8 oz. of water

Dinner: whatever the wife was making + complex carbohydrates and vegetables, 20 oz. of water

Making these simple changes not only gave him more consistent energy, more mental alertness and focus, better workouts, better body composition (he got leaner) and enhanced quality of sleep. And all of these changes were based around ADDING things in rather than cutting things out.

Looking at food as fuel also changes the way you look at your body. You will no longer expect your "machine" to function at its peak capacity if you're not giving it the fuel that it requires to do so. Depending on what you've been doing up to this point, it may be firing on a few cylinders...but it's not near maxed out. You've got another gear.

Outperform: *Eat garbage and you'll feel like garbage, which will turn your day to garbage.*

Life is a game of energy. Similar to professional athletes, Outperformers expect a lot out of their bodies. They are driven to get the most out of their days (and their life!) and are not willing to passively sit on the sidelines waiting for it to happen. Doing this takes a toll on your body and requires large energy expenditures. The only way to ensure your body is able to meet your daily demands is to give it the premium fuel that it needs.

EXERCISE

Shut Up and Train

I remember back in college, in my early fitness days, reading a muscle magazine and seeing a supplement ad that covered an entire page. There was a picture of an uber-ripped body building meathead in a tanked top and stocking hat (really, who wears that?) walking into a weight room. The ad was completely in black and white and the big bold letters at the top said "SHUT UP AND TRAIN."

Even though this chapter will have a slightly different tone, and I never tried the supplements, I've always loved that line and what (I think) the ad stood for.

Outperform: *People who train make less excuses and get better results in less time.*

When I talk to most people about "training," they think I'm just referring to athletes. I'm not. I'm referring to EVERYONE who is interested in seeing results. Exercise is for fun. Training is for getting things done. And for most people, the whole idea of exercise is about as much fun as watching paint dry. I'm bored just writing about it!

As you read this chapter, it's going to seem like I'm criticizing people who exercise. NOTHING could be further from the truth. Exercise is a great thing and the health of our country would be a lot better off if more people exercised. ANY exercise is unquestionably better than nothing at all...but we're here to Outperform The Norm, and to do that, certain shifts need to be made in your mentality and decision-making.

Now, I'm assuming you're not addicted to the snooze button and you're already putting in the time. So, what I'm really doing is showing you how two people will achieve vastly different results based on their approach to exercising vs. training.

Consider the first important distinction:

Exercisers wake up and wonder if they'll do something today. If it fits in their schedule, great. If it doesn't, that's ok too. It's a secondary priority. After all, you haven't had lunch with your friend in a while. And you've been working really hard, so you deserve to sleep in. And that weekly happy hour is always sooo much fun. You can just make up for it and exercise tomorrow, right?

Trainers write it on their calendar. In ink.

Planning when you'll train is no different than planning when you'll eat (pardon me, *feed your machine*). If you plan training around your day, it'll never get done. Or at the very least, it won't get done with the reliability necessary to be at your optimum health. It's as simple as putting it on your calendar, honoring the commitment and sticking to it.

I've seen a lot of people struggle with this aspect of training. I think part of it may be that it seems selfish to take time out of your day to do something for YOU. My response to this is that it's not about YOU – by shutting up and training, you'll not only be maximally productive because your brain will be flooded with endorphins and oxygen, you'll be that much better for everyone <u>around you</u>. You'll be a better employee or employer. Husband or wife. Father or mother. Daughter or son. Friend or colleague. You get the picture.

If you're not consistently honoring your commitment to train because you feel other things are more important, please reread the intro to this chapter. Immediately.

Now for the second important distinction:

Exercisers walk into the health club, look around, walk around, maybe chat with a few people, grab a towel, fill their water bottle, look around, walk around, go back to the locker room because they forgot their iPod, check their text messages, walk around, look around, adjust the volume on their headphones, take their headphones off so they can hear the TV, walk around, look around, walk around and eventually choose what they'll do based on where their spirit moves them...usually to the same machine where they'll exercise at the same intensity level for the same amount of time.

Trainers are purposeful with their program to measure and track what they're doing. They know that, just like in business, what gets measured gets managed. Their time is results driven. And because they can see EXACTLY where they have been previously, it becomes easy to determine if they're making progress. Numbers never lie.

Here's what I know: I've watched thousands of people in my 12+ years in health clubs. Exercisers waste time, don't see good results, aren't as motivated, aren't as consistent and aren't as happy with their overall health and fitness. Sorry – that's the harsh truth.

Outperform: *If you're not making progress, you don't know your numbers.*

Every training "session" targets a specific result. Training does NOT mean you're busting your ass at the gym 24/7. *That* would leave you overtrained and demotivated. You'd start to dread your workouts. Training means that what you're doing makes sense. There's a method to your madness. It's systematic. No guesswork.

Again, when is the last time you got in your car and drove...even though you had nowhere to go? Probably never. You get in your car and drive because you have a destination. And because you want to get there efficiently, you fire up the GPS and have it calculate the most direct route. And you flip out on those "Sunday morning" drivers hogging the road that are slowing you down and wasting your time.

Why don't you approach training this same way?

Long before I started doing marathons, I had a heavy punching bag hanging in my garage where I grew up. I convinced my parents to put it up when I was going through my "Rocky Balboa" phase. I used to beat that thing so hard that it would shake the house (GREAT stress reliever). But I was always counting the number of punches I was throwing and the number of "rounds" I could last. I'm sure any average boxer would have knocked me out in the first round and laughed at my footwork and punching combinations, but without even knowing it at the time, measuring the numbers meant I was training.

I also have numbers dating back to my first marathon in graduate school. Long runs, "tempo" runs, intervals, etc. I can see mileage, pace, heart rate and everything in between. And because I have data for such a long period of time, I can always stack up where I am now relative to where I've been in the past.

Am I always in my peak physical health? Heck no. You won't be either. Vacations happen. Illness happens. LIFE happens. And sometimes these things will throw you off course. But once you know where you've been, it's so much easier to get back there and to continue to move forward.

Training is such a simple concept, yet almost no one does it. I'm convinced that if more people trained and saw the progress they deserve to see, health clubs wouldn't have 60%+ no-show rates after 6 months. And it has nothing to do with age. You don't stop training because you get older – you get older because you stop training.

You may also be reading this thinking that I want you to be super serious in every workout, slap on your headphones, never talk to anyone and always work out alone. *That* is not the case either. You can be plenty social AND have fun when you're training – you just have to find someone who is results-driven like you are and wants to get things done.

Throughout this chapter I will show you loads of things you can measure when it comes to training. And, theoretically, anything you measure, as long as it's going in a positive direction, will translate to results. You just have to be willing to track it and stick with it.

Minimum Effective Dose (MED)

Once you've got the "shut up and train" mindset in place, the next part is to understand what *really* counts when it comes to exercise. Many people have the mentality that if you cannot work out for at least 45-60 minutes, it's not beneficial. That's BS. The Surgeon General is always putting out reports on how they recommend, "45-60 minutes of moderate intensity exercise, 5 times per week." First off, I don't even know what "moderate intensity" is. Second, if you can get the same benefits from doing less of something, isn't that what you should be after?

This term is used by a surprisingly few number of people in the fitness industry. I first heard it used from Dr. John Berrardi of Precision

Nutrition and it's also mentioned by Tim Ferriss in *The 4 Hour Body*.

The simplest way to look at the MED is like prescription medication; which are all based around the MED. When doctors prescribe a medication, they know if they don't prescribe a strong enough dosage, you won't see the benefits. They also know if they prescribe too strong a dosage, you will probably get side effects. Thus, their job is to prescribe the precise dosage that will a) be strong enough to elicit the benefit needed, and b) not have negative consequences by an unnecessarily high prescription.

These are the exact principles of the MED.

Now, the way that exercise differs from the MED is that you're not likely to receive ANY negative consequences from exercising too much (unless you get into extreme cases of exercise addiction and dependency). But this is the exact model is used to work with athletes and non-athletes. This is going to sound odd to say, but I personally don't love exercise. I don't look forward to it. I don't jump out of bed at 5am on a cold morning *dying* to exercise. The intrinsic *process* of exercise is not appealing to me.

What I crave is the RESULT. I want to feel, think, look, act and perform better on a daily basis and THAT is why I do it. For the most part, while I'm doing it, I'm often thinking about other things...and waiting for it to be done (maybe you can relate?). It's a means to an end.

Outperform: *Exercise is the most potent performance-enhancing drug for your life.*

If you're anything like me, the MED is perfect for you. Exercise is the most powerful drug you can possibly take to get better results in your life. Period. Take it. And take it often. Because my main objective with exercise is for it to enhance other areas of my life, I'm not concerned with going above and beyond the call of duty. I want the maximum benefits in the minimum amount of time.

Because of this, I will not do more than I have to...at least not in terms of duration. Why would I? If I can get the same benefits from a 30-mile bike ride, why am I going to ride 50 miles? If I can get the same strength training benefits from a 30-minute pump, why am I going to train for 45 minutes?
This is actually a surprising contrast to many people I come across. Most people are addicted to duration and think that more is always better...and necessary.

Consistency

Outperform: *We are what we repeatedly do (thank you, Aristotle).*

The single most important component of your exercise program is *consistency*. We are what we repeatedly do. Without consistency in something, none of the other variables matter.

Consistency can be synonymous with frequency, and they both relate to how often you do something (usually measured in terms of how many times per week). And the proper consistency for an Outperforming exercise program is 6-7 times per week. Yes, you read that correctly – that could mean exercising everyday. If exercise were a drug, why would you NOT take it everyday?

I used to travel often for my previous sales job and I got very accustomed to staying in hotels. Now, you come to realize that, despite every hotel claiming to have a "state of the art fitness center," it usually falls a little short of your expectations. Thus, I'd have to get VERY creative with my workouts at hotels to make sure I kept up with my consistency.

Outperform: *You have early morning meetings? Fine. Get up even earlier.*

I used to meet with a lot of schools and the best time to meet with teachers is *before* classes actually start. This means most meetings would start between 7:00-7:30am, which means I'd have to leave my hotel by 6:45ish, be eating breakfast by 6:30, be in the shower by 6:00, be done working out by 5:55, be starting my workout by 5:15-5:30 (depending on the type of workout), which means the alarm was probably set for 5:00am.

What's the big problem? Get out of bed earlier.

Most people who travel (or are thrown out of their routine in general) miss workouts. Could I have taken days off when I was traveling? Sure. But that's the excuse everyone makes. And I've found a common characteristic of highly successful people to be the willingness to get up early and do what it takes to stay in their routine.

This is an example cycle that normally happens: let's say I'm traveling for 4 days. The first day I have an early morning meeting and I don't get up to hammer my exercise drug. Then, I don't eat as well at breakfast. Then, I don't feel my best so I don't eat well at lunch. Then, I really feel like crap so the typical minor inconveniences become major stressors throughout the day. By the time I get back to the hotel, I'm tired, stressed, not feeling well and the best thing seems to be to belly up to the hotel bar, order a big slab of beef with a fat-filled appetizer and eat my emotional stress away. After a couple drinks of liquid medication, I stumble up to my room where I sleep like garbage, which gives me the golden excuse to skip my morning workout the next day because I'm just too tired.

Outperform: *Hotel beds are comfortable. It is your body that is uncomfortable.*

This entire cycle could have been altered by one MED of exercise in the morning. Simple as that.

Vicious cycles like this happen all the time and they WRECK our consistency. Again, we are what we repeatedly do, for better or for worse. Once you're in a consistent exercise routine, it's SO much easier to stay in it. But once you get out of it, you've got the ball rolling the other direction and it's THAT much more difficult to turn it around.

Another benefit of a consistent exercise routine is that your body starts to crave it. Even if your mind doesn't *want* to do it (like mine doesn't), your body *craves* the results. If you go a few days without it, you start to have an itchy feeling where something isn't quite right. This is how you adopt a consistent, Outperforming pattern of exercise.

Progressive Overload (Intensity)

Ask any trainer, coach, strength & conditioning specialist, or otherwise, what the most important component is in an exercise program and they will tell you progressive overload.

You show me someone who is not making progress; I'll show you someone who's not employing progressive overload.

Technical definition is: "gradual increase of stress placed upon the body during exercise training."

Layman's definition is: "keep doing greater intensities than you're doing and you'll see results."

Problem is, what exactly constitutes *"greater?"*

If you're an endurance athlete, you'll get these examples – if you want to improve your running, you HAVE TO do one (or more) of the following:

a) Run faster
b) Run more often
c) Run longer
d) Run more volume (total weekly mileage)

Any of these things will equal progressive overload in a weekly program. If you want to go into progressive overload in a single training session, this is another can of worms. Then it's more intervals, faster intervals, longer intervals, shorter rest periods, etc. These same examples of exercise can apply to any form of cardiovascular exercise.

Most people do not understand progressive overload and intensity in training. It DOES NOT just mean lifting heavier weights (though this is one way to create progressive overload). If you're looking to make gains, increase tone, balance, stability, strength, power, endurance, or whatever else, you need to manipulate training intensity, which is how difficult something is, or how much energy it takes to accomplish something.

Here are examples of creating progressive overload in a training program:

1. Lift heavier weights. A dichotomy usually exists between men and women. Men normally lift weights that are too heavy for them to do with proper form. It's a macho thing. Women normally don't lift weights heavy *enough* because they are afraid of "getting big." But rest assured ladies, unless you start injecting testosterone, 99% of you are incapable of putting on significant muscle mass...regardless of how heavy you lift.

2. Decrease rest periods. Less time between sets and exercises.

3. Increase number of sets. If you're doing 2 sets of every exercise now, 3 sets will create progressive overload.

4. Increase number of repetitions. If you're doing 15 reps of every exercise now, 20 reps will create progressive overload.

5. Increase number of exercises. If your overall program has 8 total exercises you're doing, 10 will create progressive overload.

6. Increase training frequency. If you strength train 2x/week right now, 3x/week will create progressive overload.

7. Increase difficulty of exercises. Simplest way to see this: 1) do a pushup with your hands on a bench and feet on the floor, 2) do a regular pushup, 3) do a pushup with your hands on the floor and feet on a bench. You'll see instantly which one is the most challenging. Lever angles and subtle changes can make all exercises easier or more difficult.

8. Increase the speed of the exercise. If you always do your exercises in a 2:2 ratio (sec: sec), performing your exercises faster will create progressive overload.

Now, PLEASE do not try to manipulate any more than 1-2 of these factors at any given time. If you try to add in all these things at once you're going to be lying in the fetal position on your bathroom floor. Baby steps.

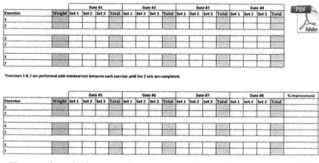

*Download the workout template that I use with clients at the **Outperformer's Vault**.*

OutperformTheNorm.com/Vault

This is a simple excel spreadsheet creates progressive overload and calculates totals and % improvement. After you've downloaded it, complete it using the following:

- Choose 6 exercises and keep them constant for all 8 sessions
- Keep weight, rest periods and speed of exercises constant for all 8 sessions as well
- In each workout, try to do more reps than you did in the previous workout

This is as simple as it gets. But, please be aware that this is ONLY going to target muscular endurance, which may or may not be your limiting factor in strength training. I would have to write a novel to encompass all the different ways of switching things around to achieve specific results.

The reason intensity is such a critical factor is that our bodies are constantly adapting to what we're doing. Here's what most people don't realize about training – if you're not doing *anything* right now and you start doing *something* (it honestly doesn't matter what it is), you'll see results. The quality of the results will depend on the relative intensity of what you're doing. But you'll see gains simply by doing more than you're doing at the current moment...which is *anything*.

However, once you get past an initial acclimation period (about 3 weeks) your body will start to adapt. At this point, doing the same thing over and over and over again will no longer produce results. The only way to continue to see progress is to shock your system with greater intensity.

If you're someone who has been working out regularly, intensity is the key (and the ONLY way) you will take your training, and fitness, to the next level. For experienced exercisers, this is usually the first variable I look at. They already have established the consistency but they are no longer manipulating the intensity to the degree that will produce results.

Outperform: *If it seems like I'm telling you to work out harder, GOOD. I am.*

Duration

Duration is the total amount of time you spend training and most people think it is the most important factor in a workout. I cannot possibly tell you the number of people, men and women, who say they work out at least 90 minutes every time they go to the gym. 90 minutes? *Doing what?* They assume if their workout is longer then mine; it must be better, right?

Not necessarily.

Is a 45-minute training session better than 30 minutes? Probably. But, first you have to look at the consistency. Are these workouts happening at least six times per week? If so, you've passed checkpoint #1.

Next, are these workouts at the proper intensities to see results based on your training history and your current consistency? Are you training *hard enough* to reap the benefits? If so, you've passed checkpoint #2.

But this is where the tradeoff usually happens – if you train harder, your durations are shorter. If you train easier, your durations are longer. Nobody can train extremely hard for 90 minutes. It doesn't matter how fit you are.

Now, I'm not saying that you should do hard, short workouts every time you train. There are definite aerobic and fat-burning benefits to working out for longer durations and lower intensities. But, I'm assuming you're reading this book because you're a bit like me – you crave the *results* you get from training, and the reason you want these results is because you have a desire to Outperform in many areas outside the gym (personally, professionally, etc.). If this is the case, why spend more time than you have to get the same results? Get it done and get out.

At checkpoint #3 comes duration. Assuming you've passed the first two checkpoints, then sure, longer durations almost always trump shorter durations. But this SHOULD NOT be your primary focus when looking at a training program. Establish consistency and intensity *first*...then worry about duration.

A Case Study In Outperforming Health

The first thing I do anytime I have a new client is to take about 30 minutes to discuss their goals and exactly *what* we are going to accomplish, *when* we are going to accomplish it by and *why* they want to accomplish it. Based on this information, it is my job to come up with the *how* it will get accomplished.

In this case, Carl's initial goal was to lose 15 pounds in the next two months. Easily doable. He has a heavy travel schedule and the extra weight has left him feeling tired and sluggish towards the end of his workdays, which makes it difficult for him to be maximally productive in late afternoon and evening meetings.

When going over his lifestyle and fitness routine, this is what I heard (summarized):

"I work out 3-4x per week and do a total body program of about 12 exercises. Mostly upper body, abs and cardio. I typically use the machines. Cardio is mostly on the elliptical. I eat about 3x per day and drink 1-2 glasses of water per day. I don't sleep that well at night."

First, I'm not being critical of what he's doing. In fact, it's the NORM. This is a very typical outline of someone who has been working out for a while but is simply not doing the correct things to maximize their results.

Second, I knew he was going to be successful and lose 15 pounds. How could I be so sure? Because he already had the majority of the patterns and routines ingrained in his behavior. He was just barely offline but a slight correction would put him back on course.

Here are the simple tweaks I made:

- **Strength train the legs.** Why? The legs are the largest muscle group in the body. Work them and you'll burn more calories. More calories burned equals more weight loss. You get more bang for your buck.

- **Less machines, more free weights and exercises where you have to support your own body weight.** The problem with using traditional machines is that you're almost always sitting. We sit enough in our daily lives – get up! Engaging your smaller stabilizer muscles while standing and having freedom of movement in these exercises also increases caloric burn.

- **Fewer exercises.** More quality, less quantity. You don't need to hit the smaller muscles as hard (arms, abs, calves, etc.) if you're hitting the big muscle groups (legs, back, chest) first. My workouts normally don't include more than 6-8 exercises, total (again, see the template in the **Outperformer's Vault).** And I'm smoked afterwards. A few key exercises done at the *proper* intensities are all you need.

- **Cardio on the treadmill.** He has no previous history of lower extremity injuries so we may as well maximize his time doing cardio. Treadmill always trumps elliptical because you have to support more of your own body weight and move it through space. Stairmaster is the same way (better than elliptical). The more freedom of movement you have, the more calories you will burn...and they more weight you'll lose.

- **1-2 more meals per day.** He needs to be eating 4-5 times per day to create a steady burning metabolism. Convenience is key because he travels. So, we decided he'd carry an extra 1-2 Meal Replacement Shakes with him each day. A meal replacement bar would have also been a solid option. It simply depends on whether you want to drink something or chew something.

- **More water.** I told him to bring a water bottle, and like a good soldier, he walked in with a brand new 34-ounce bottle. I told him starting out, the minimum was to drink 2 of those per day and it should never leave his side. 68 ounces is just a starting point that we'll add to over time. This will maximize nutrient transport and toxin removal in his body.

- **Try to adopt a sleeping routine**. The best way to do this is to go to bed at the same time every night. Much of sleep is finding your own individual pattern and sticking to it…long-term (I'm preaching to myself on this one). Sleeping is no different than any other routine in your life. Once it is created, you'll find it much easier to stick to it.

Once Carl made these changes, he had a burning metabolism like he hadn't seen in a loooong time. And the beautiful thing about it is that I didn't ask him to do anything dramatically *different* from what he has been doing. If anything, I simplified the process.

Outperform: *The difference between Outperform and The Norm is often one degree.*

You've probably heard the popular line: "*At 211 degrees water is hot; at 212 degrees it boils. That one degree makes all the difference.*" In his case, that one-degree resulted in him achieving his goals. We didn't have to reinvent the wheel. We didn't have to carve out time for him to add in exercise. He was already doing these things – I just gave him the strategies to move his health, fitness and body composition to the next level…all by shifting that one degree.

RECOVERY

Hack the Aging Process

Since the summer after my senior year of high school I've had people tell me the following:

- When you get to college you'll gain weight (the "Freshman 15") because you'll always be drinking
- When you get to grad school you'll gain weight because you'll always be studying
- When you graduate you'll gain weight because you'll always be working
- When you take this sales job, you'll gain weight because you'll always be traveling
- When you take this management job, you'll gain weight because you'll always be sitting
- When you get to 25…or 30…you'll gain weight because your metabolism starts slowing

Despite what I've heard, I've never gained weight. Now I'm 33 and I sometimes hear the following:

- When you get to 35...40...45...50...(you know the rest)

Where does it stop?

Outperform: *Stop using the number of years you've been on this planet as an excuse.*

Want to know the truth? From a health and fitness perspective, only two primary things decline with age:

- After the ages of 25-30 (studies are conflicted), you'll lose 0.5-1% of muscle mass each year.
- Your body doesn't recover as quickly from intense workouts.

Now, we're all getting older. Let's accept it. It's a fact of life. Almost everyone reading this book (age 25+) is in a period of decline. From a purely biological perspective, my bones and muscles and organs and glands will all be older next year than they are right now.

I'll also be the first to admit that there are *certain things* we cannot do as we age. Case in point – way back in the day I LOVED McDonald's, and I would always get the same thing – Double Quarter Pounder with Cheese, Supersized Fries, Large Chocolate Shake. And I would go play sports *afterwards*!

(Oh, to be young and athletic)

If I tried to do that now, I'd be a wheezing heart attack waiting to happen (not that I ever would). I'd be hands-on-knees in the first minute.

But some of these statistics can be misleading. Losing muscle mass with age is measured by taking muscle biopsy samples of the same person doing the same thing over and over across time.

This is what people don't realize: you getting older + insanity (doing the same thing over and over) = decline in muscle mass.

It doesn't have to be this way.

Outperform: *Continuously challenging your body defies the aging process.*

I'm fortunate to have worked with a large clientele of people over 40. All of them are getting better with age…and all of them will CONTINUE to get better. Heck, if they can put up with me for long enough, they'll probably still be getting better…even into their 50's!

If you're reading this book saying, *"but Scott, you just don't know what it's like,"* you're right – I don't. I have absolutely no idea. I don't know where you are and I haven't been where you've been.

I'll never forget being at a happy hour a few years ago when an older woman started debating me on this point. Her argument: "you don't know what it's like to be a woman and be [insert older age, I can't remember what it was]." Isn't that kind of an unfair argument? I could have easily responded with "you don't know what it's like to be a man." There is nothing you can say to that.

All I know is what statistics say, what I've experienced, what I've seen and what I believe. Here it is:

The average American gains about 1 pound per year. And most don't gain it because of aging – they gain it because of their own lifestyle CHOICES. They are more sedentary. They move less. They watch too much TV. They eat more. Their foods are too processed. They drink more. They exercise less.

Outperform: *People gain weight because of their own choices. It has little to do with aging.*

Every single person reading this needs to know that you CAN get better with age and continuous improvement is not only possible, it's *probable*, if you manipulate a small number of easily manageable variables…notably exercise, nutrition, sleep and stress. I've seen it happen before and I will help others do it again.

So, this chapter on recovery starts by keepin' it real – with <u>yourself</u>. If you've been using age as a crutch for your own unhealthy lifestyle circumstances, please stop. Immediately. Step up and be held accountable. You are capable of much, much more.

Stress

Stress is, literally, killing our society. Many people spend their days in a constant fight-or-flight state based on our accelerated daily responsibilities and obligations. This response causes hormonal spikes that are ruining the ability of our glands to properly function. Stress can cause major damage to your health, mood, productivity, relationships and overall quality of life.

Perception is Reality

The starting point to combating stress lies in our *perception* of events. Think about it, before something can be deemed stressful, it has to be perceived a certain way. Our perception determines our reality.

When you head into an important meeting with a prospective client, how you view this meeting will have a MAJOR effect on your stress level. Are you confident or hesitant? Prepared or unorganized? Clear headed or cloudy? Is the sale life or death (yes, based on your perception, this may be a valid question)?

Outperform: *Your perception becomes your reality.*

Negative perception is almost always caused by a lack of belief. Most of the time this is a lack of belief in your own talents, skills or abilities. This lack of belief causes stress anytime you need to rise up to meet a challenge because you question whether you have what it takes to get the job done.

So, anti-stress training should first start with belief in yourself. If you believe that you have the answers and the wherewithal to accomplish whatever you set your mind to, it will immediately decrease stress the next time a potentially negative event arises.

Negative perception could also be caused by your circumstantial beliefs. These beliefs stem from feeling like you don't possess the resources demanded in a certain situation, such as the ability to get out of debt...or the strength to make a difficult decision. But, by far the biggest circumstantial belief comes believing there is too much to do and not enough time, which makes you perceive a great deal of stress. Time management skills and learning to become a better investment manager of what's *important* vs. what is *urgent* (covered later) is necessary if you want to get out of the "me vs. time" game.

Otherwise, you're going to be in a constant tug-of-war with you against time. Whoever pulls harder, wins. And usually, there is so much stacked up against you that time almost always wins. Time is always a finite commodity but there is no limit for the buildup of demands.

In the case of sales and business, stress is usually caused by a lack of belief in your product or company (in addition to some of the beliefs mentioned already). The only way you have to deal with professional stress is to increasingly buy in to your company's mission or vision, and to the valuable benefits your product can provide to society. Believe this and you'll no longer perceive the same level of stress. You'll simply be making a confident recommendation based on what you *honestly* believe is in the best interest of the consumer.

I've managed people in sales almost all my life. Many of the people who "aren't good at sales," are good people and are excellent communicators. What they're missing is the confidence gene (the gene that turns *everything* around). They lack confidence.

People don't buy products. People buy confidence. Increasing your confidence will increase the number of people who buy from you. It has nothing to do with sales. It has to do with how much you believe in yourself. And if you're reading this thinking it doesn't apply to you because you don't work in sales – it still does. *Everyone* is selling something...even if you're selling an idea or your influence. It pays to have confidence in ALL situations.

I'm spending so much time on confidence and self-belief because these things have everything to do with your negative perception of events and you telling yourself, "I can't do it. I'm not good enough. I'm not ready. I'm not able."

Outperform: *Outperformers don't stress because they can handle ANYTHING.*

So, what causes a faulty perception and causes you to get stressed?

Chronic Pessimism

I just glanced out the window. It's "kinda sunny." I have two choices on what I see:

1 – It's partly sunny

2 – It's mostly cloudy

One emphasizes the positive. One emphasizes the negative.

I'm also halfway through my glass of water.

1 – The glass is half full

2 – The glass is half empty

Yes, this is painfully simple, but if it's so simple, why don't we do it more often? The great majority of things in life ARE simpler than we realize. Pay attention to the lens with which you see the world. Constantly emphasizing what's *wrong* before (or instead of) emphasizing what's *right*, will lead to increased stress.

Inability to Accept Uncertainty and Change

Change is a fact of life. Deal with it. The world around us is changing so fast and almost nothing stays the same. Technology, business, relationships, health, weather, etc. – none of it ever remains static.

All of these things progress or regress. They never maintain.

People who are chronically stressed are not able to deal with change and uncertainty as well as others. Why? Because they see any change that happens as automatically being *worse* than their current situation.

Less stressed people see uncertainty and change as potentially *better*. They know there is magic on the other side of change.

Negative Self Talk

What you say to yourself matters. In the sports world today, an increasing number of players and coaches are getting "mic'ed up," where they periodically wear a microphone so the everyday sports fan can get a glimpse of what is actually said in the heat of competition. It makes fans feel like they're part of the action.

Outperform: *The Norm has 60,000 thoughts per day and 80% of them are negative.*

What if you were mic'ed up everyday, not for what you say to others but what you say to YOURSELF? Would you be proud of it? Would you be comfortable putting it out there for the world to hear? Would you want your kids or spouse to hear it?

Most people would say heck no.

What you would tolerate from others is no different than what you should tolerate from yourself. If you wouldn't tolerate someone telling you that you're fat, ugly, stupid, incapable, hopeless, afraid and worthless, then stop tolerating it from yourself. Demand better. Demand that the way you speak to yourself is exactly the same as you would want someone else speaking to you. You deserve that.

Unrealistic Expectations

I normally subscribe to the philosophy, "Shoot for the stars. Even if you don't make it, at least you'll land on the moon." Normally, this is a good strategy. Lofty goals are important.

Where it becomes a bad strategy is when your expectations of getting to the stars are unrealistic. You either want to get there too fast or have no idea how to get it done. When this happens, you're bound to get stressed. Better to scale back the expectation to something that is challenging, yet realistic.

Perfectionism

Perfectionists demand flawlessness and have extremely high performance standards. Most people know this side of perfectionism. Many successful athletes and business leaders are wired this way.

The side of perfectionism that many don't know is that perfectionists are not only critical in their self-evaluations, but they are also overly concerned by the evaluations of others. This leads many perfectionists to become stressed when they feel they're letting themselves (and others) down. This stress can eventually lead to depression when you're not living up to high standards.

Lack of Assertiveness

"DO SOMETHING!"

My mom used to always tell me that when I was younger. If I was walking around the house, bored or sad or stressed, it was her typical response.

Outperform: *Massive action solves all problems.*

Unassertiveness causes stress because, instead of DOING something, you are sitting around dwelling...usually on the negative aspects of whatever is wrong. And because no forward motion is being made towards getting out, it makes you feel like you'll always be stuck there.

Now that you understand what's making you stressed and how your perception of events is everything, it still pays to know how to cope when you become stressed. Here's what you can do about it:

Imagery

Your imagination is a POWERFUL thing and, in the right circumstances, can be used to your advantage against stress. It gets you wishing, wondering what is out there. Imagining what can be.

Imagery is crucial in sport psychology and mental training. If an athlete cannot see himself (or herself) making the game-winning shot, kicking the game-winning field goal, or making the tournament-winning putt, it's not going to happen. Seeing is believing.

I always say sport psychology is *life psychology* – it is simply more specialized towards athletes. The concepts of imagining and imagery are every bit as important and applicable to life as they are to athletics.

Outperform: *If you cannot see it happen in your mind, it will NEVER happen in reality.*

Let's take the popular weight loss example –
say you really want to lose weight but the
pounds aren't coming off. You're stressed,
frustrated and thinking about quitting. You
can give up and do any of these things OR you
can use imagery to decrease stress and enhance
motivation.

Some questions for you…

- Can you see yourself looking into the
  mirror with a reflection that's 10-15 lbs.
  lighter?
- How is it going to feel when you're able
  to wear clothes that haven't fit in years?
- What will it mean to you to have people
  complimenting you left and right on
  how great you look?
- How is weight loss going to change
  your attitude? How will you feel about
  yourself as a person?
- Can you imagine having energy to do
  ALL the things you want to do…from
  sun up to sun down?

You want to know a key to less stress and more
motivation? There it is…plain and simple.
Don't *think* about what you're going to get
done – IMAGINE what that's going to *do for
you*.

Let me let you in on a little secret – people do
not want to lose weight, have more energy or

make more money. They want what's underneath the hood. They want the feeling.

One thing essential about imagery is to incorporate as many of the senses as possible. Think about the last time you were driving along in your car and heard a song that reminded you of something. I'll bet what you remembered wasn't some ordinary, run of the mill day. It contained an emotional component and you were able to recall incredibly vivid details. What it looked like…felt like…smelled like…tasted like…sounded like.

Imagery is no different – it is simply taking this level of vivid detail and applying it to the <u>future</u> instead of the past. And if something in the present is stressing you out and you want to get something done in the future, create an emotional attachment to it. IMAGINE IT. See the specifics. The same way that unassertiveness causes stress, imagery will move you. Forward. You will do something.

Outperform: *Nothing great ever happens without first seeing it in your mind.*

Every now and then I get asked what I think about during long hours of training for Ironman...when I'm frustrated and stressed and thinking about quitting (yes, this happens to me too). The answer is simple – I think about how it is going to FEEL crossing the finish line. And when I think about it, I can hear the crowd cheering and announcer calling my name. I can taste and smell the sweat (gross!). But most of all, I imagine the deep sense of pride and satisfaction I'll have from trying my best and accomplishing a goal. Sometimes I get emotional during training just thinking about it.

I may not know a lot, but I do know that passion and drive and change and growth and accomplishments and risks and rewards and realizations and successes beyond comprehension are NOT grown from logic – they're grown from emotion. Trust me – there is NOTHING logical about Ironman (why in the heck would you want to do 140.6 miles in a day, anyway?). It's ok to let yourself be emotional! Living your entire life being "logical," can lead you to be paralyzed by fear instead of driven by desire.

So, what is stressing you out? Can you see your way out? Can you *REALLY* see it? How will it feel? What will it do for you? Are you able to imagine it?

Support Network

Stress can happen from being alone and having no support network. People want to be around other people. I love my dog and she's a great supporter (aren't all dogs, though?) but nothing replaces a solid human support network. They allow you to vent your stresses and frustrations.

On the other hand, stress can also happen from having the *wrong* support network. Surrounding yourself with people who are negative and do nothing but pull you down won't relieve stress. They will contribute to it.

Lastly, a social network is not a legitimate support network. Yes, I know, that woe-is-me stressed out Facebook post got 98 likes and 37 comments...but did it REALLY make you feel better? Wouldn't it be better to have coffee or dinner with a few close friends and be supported face to face? People need people.

Sense of Control

Think about it – the things that stress you out are the things that are out of your control. If something is 100% in your control, you feel no stress. You've got this.

Faith is an important component of stress management. There is always only so much you can control in life. You should strive to control what you can control and leave the rest up to faith.

When you do a triathlon there are many unknowns. Newbie triathletes think they can control everything (which they can't). The only real controllables in racing are your preparation, attitude and effort. The rest is outside of you...and this is what causes the majority of stress. I've had goggles break on the swim, tires go flat on the bike, shoes come apart on the run and an upset stomach even though I'd eaten the same foods hundreds of times without issue. Sometimes, sh*t just HAPPENS.

Life is no different. Control how you prepare for a given situation, your attitude and how you'll respond to adversity and the amount of effort you're willing to give. If you focus on these 3 key areas, you will notice your stress immediately decrease.

Ability to Manage Your Emotions

Think of the least stressed people you know – they're probably very "Steady Eddy," right? Never too high, never too low? Always on an even keel?

Then think of the most stressed people you know – they're probably like a volcano - volatile, and ready to erupt at moment's notice.

Most people think that stress causes you to erupt, but is it possible that it works the other way around? That maybe your inability to control your emotions is making you more stressed?

Outperform: *Stress happens BECAUSE of dramatic mood swings, not as a result of it.*

Yes, this is true. Control your emotions and you'll control your stress level. Boring as it sounds, the best way to relieve stress is remain as level as possible throughout the course of the day. Just like your car, there will be less wear and tear if you drive a constant speed than if you're constantly slamming on the gas and brakes.

Knowledge and Preparation

Outperform: *Failing to prepare is preparing to fail.*

Americans consistently rank public speaking as the thing they fear the most. This could be because they're paranoid of being judged and evaluated, or maybe they're just not very good at picturing the crowd naked and in black socks (hopefully I'm not the only one who ever heard that trick!).

But the *real* reason most Americans are stressed by public speaking is that they simply haven't done it enough. ANYTIME you attempt to do something you haven't done, it's going to be stressful. We're creatures of habit and we don't like the unfamiliar. Just the act of doing something we haven't done causes most of us stress...especially if it's something we're being *forced* to do (like giving a presentation at work) versus something that we're *choosing* to do (like vacationing somewhere unfamiliar).

In this case, the best way to combat stress is to gather as much knowledge as possible and prepare. Acquiring knowledge and preparing to the best of your ability builds familiarity. And familiarity bolsters stress.

Is that test stressing you out? Study harder. Are you nervous about your proposal at work? Practice more. Are you worried that your company is going to downsize? Research other opportunities.

These simple responses will cure your stress.

I started this chapter talking about *The Gap* between what we know and what we do. Now that you know what it takes to achieve Outperforming health, are you going to DO IT? Are you going to take massive action?

You can read every health book in the bookstore and it won't make a darn difference if you don't *apply* what you're learned. This isn't health through osmosis. The acquisition of knowledge is useless without the application of it.

Outperform: *Implementing 10% of this chapter will improve your life by 100%.*

If you do this, there's nothing stopping you. You'll look better, feel better and perform better immediately...and over the long haul. You will be free from illness and injury (God willing), but more importantly, *every* aspect of your life will soar to another level (possibly one you've never seen before). You won't believe the improvements in your productivity and your personal relationships. You'll be living an Outperforming life.

OUTPERFORM NOW: Health

1. Decide what you'll have for breakfast, starting *tomorrow*. Buy whatever foods you need to tonight and budget time if you're planning to cook. Include protein and have within 30 minutes of waking up, or within 30 minutes of finishing your morning training.

2. What foods are you committed to eating more of? Pick a few from each of the 5 categories and write them down. Go buy them...TODAY. Also buy a case of water and a new water bottle while you're at it.

3. What will you do to shape your environment to make Outperforming as easy as possible, for nutrition, exercise or stress? What *simple* tweaks could you make that would yield massive long results?

4. If you eat garbage, the next time garbage tempts you, stop and write down exactly how you're going to feel AFTER eating it. Break your pattern of eating on impulse. Link the after effects. The more vivid and graphic you can describe the crappy feelings, the better.

5. What are your training goals? What do you want to weigh? What do you want your body

composition at? How strong do you want to be? Next, determine what the realistic MED is for you to get those things done. Then put it into your schedule. In ink.

6. What one area are you going to target to create progressive overload in your training program? In your life? In what ways are you coasting and no longer challenging yourself?

7. What are the main sources of your stress? What are you focused on? How can you shift your perception to offload some of this stress?

8. What do you say to yourself every day...personally and professionally? Write it down. Change it if it's not something that you would let anyone else say to you.

9. Imagine your perfect health and perfect life – what does it look like? What do you have? How does it make you feel? What does it allow you to do that you cannot do right now? Write a mission statement for your health and life...in the *present tense*. For example, "I exercise every day and live vibrantly and without stress." Your mind will find a way to make it happen.

10. What is your support network for stress? Family? Friends? Co-workers? Pets? Identify them and have them hold you accountable for keeping your stress in check. Let me know how that works out with the pets :)

HIGH PERFORMANCE

I love cars.

In 2005, my dad was working for Pontiac and they brought back the GTO, which, in the late 1960's and early 1970's, was your stereotypical "muscle car." And, even though I was a broke graduate student, I got a killer deal on a 2-year lease of a GTO. Considering my previous car was a Plymouth Sundance where I had duct taped the bumper to keep it from falling off, this was a SERIOUS upgrade. I was a kid in a candy store.

The GTO had a 5.7-liter V8 engine with 400 horsepower that went 0-60 in 4.6 seconds. That beast had throttle like you wouldn't believe! I'd blink and I'd be at 100mph (please don't tell my mom...or law enforcement).

Now THAT is high performance.

Think if you could get your body...your business...your LIFE to function at that level of performance? Every time you want to get to your next destination faster, you barely tap the gas and you have *massive* forward acceleration. You'd be unstoppable!

The trouble is, we are our own biggest obstacles. We get in our own way...mostly with our mind.

Outperform: *Our mind can either be our greatest asset or our largest liability.*

Real life conversations that I've had with, literally, hundreds of clients...

"You're going to do...[insert something really difficult]*."*

"I CAN'T do that," they respond.

"YES, you can," I reply.

Simple story, right? In 12+ years in the health and personal development industries, I've NEVER had a client not be able to do something I asked them to do. They ALL do it...once I assure them they CAN. But, before I told them this, they didn't believe it and they tried to talk themselves out of it. Their limiting beliefs become a self-fulfilling prophecy.

It strikes me that this is such a common reaction whenever a very difficult potential obstacle is put in our path. How often have you wanted to do something such as start a business, try a diet, ask someone out, join a group, do a race, climb a mountain, or be adventurous and you talked yourself out of it because you didn't think you could do it?

I also find it interesting that my clients who DON'T have this reaction are also the most successful in other aspects of their life, namely business. Most are executives, entrepreneurs, business owners or top sales managers. Their mindset towards what they can accomplish in health and fitness obviously has served them well elsewhere. Their attitude is not situation-specific – they carry it in all areas.

You've probably heard the quote that *"whether you think you can or think you can't, you're right."* It's absolutely true. I can tell you with 100% conclusive certainty that if you cannot see it happen in your mind, it will not happen in reality. This is why all high level athletes practice imagery. High performance starts with your mindset...and when you can remove any self-imposed limitations you have on yourself by first seeing it in your *mind*; your performance in *reality* goes to another level. You've lifted the governor on your GTO. You'll be doing 100mph in no time!

High performance is actually not as difficult, or complex, as it may seem. Now that you have your health finely tuned and your soul filled with happiness, all that it takes for high performance is the proper mindset, the desire to get the process started and a "can do, will do" attitude. This will get you to *periods* of high performance, or the ability to raise your game on command.

But if you want to SUSTAIN that level of performance (which, I think is what everyone is looking for), consistently, long-term, you need knowledge and mastery of the fundamentals, and the durability to stand the test of time. Even a Pontiac GTO is no good if it breaks down on the open road.

MINDSET

Consider. It. Done.

Imagine you're living on an island. On this island are safety, security and the "comfortable life." Nothing much changes here. You know what to expect day-in and day-out. Storms rarely come and the weather is satisfactory.

This island is heavily populated because it's the status quo. *The Norm.* People work 8-5, collect their checks and pay their bills. Daily life is busy with everything that is urgent and little that is important. It is easy but feels monotonous, which is why the island is rampant with artificial energy drinks. The juice of life isn't giving them what they need.

In the far distance is another island. On this island are passion and purpose and abundance and an insatiable zest for life. You've heard about this island but you've never experienced it. You know some people who have been there. You may be envious...or possibly even resent them for it. But you can't help wonder what it's like. You wonder whether you'd belong...or whether it's worth it.

This island is volatile. Storms are uncertain and come at a moment's notice. But they always blow through, and when they do, the weather is more glorious than anything you can possibly imagine. It's a lot less crowded on this island and there is a lot more to go around. People passionately work their asses off and are rewarded handsomely for it. There is an unspoken truth for people on this island – they've paid *The Price of Admission*. It doesn't need to be said; it's just understood.

On the shore of the comfortable island is a boat with your name on it. At any point you can make the DECISION to travel to the other island...with only one condition: once you get there, you have to burn the boat.

Outperform: *If you WANT the island, you've got to BURN the boat. No exceptions.*

This means when you go, you stay. No turning back. It doesn't matter how bad the storms get – you don't leave. Ever. You're committed to staying there because you've burned the fricken' boat – your only means of transportation back. Any mention of going back to your Plan B safety net of a comfortable, "really busy," someday-I-will-do-it, paycheck-to-paycheck, artificially enhanced existence on the other island is gone. That's what it takes to get to this island.

Will you come aboard?

Outperform: *Plan B's don't exist when you're fully committed to your Plan A.*

In all the work I've done with high performing athletes (regardless of sport), it always strikes me that people THINK the biggest difference between Outperformers and The Norm is innate talent. It's the "I wasn't born with that" mentality and it's BS. A total cop out. Read any book on neuroplasticity, behavioral conditioning, motor learning and skill development and you'll realize that high performers have simply WORKED that much harder to refine their skills. They made the decision to travel to the island and they have spent thousands of hours weathering the storms. Yes, talent is important, but it is *given*. Skills are *earned* by blood and sweat and tears and being in the trenches. And highly developed skills will always produce better results (in business, athletics or otherwise) than any amount of natural talent.

What allows high performers to develop these skills is their MINDSET. Here's the breakdown:

The Norm	Outperformers
Hopefully	Definitely
Probably	Definitely
Maybe	Definitely
I think	I will
I hope	I will
I might	I will
I'll try	I'll succeed
I'll see what I can do	I'll do it
When I have time	I'll make time
If it happens	I'll make it happen
I blame you	I'm responsible
Excuses	Accountability
Not sure	Certainty
Comfortable	Challenged
Safety	Adventure
Secure decisions	Calculated risks
Resources	Resourcefulness
Given	Earned
Easy way	Best way
Later	Now
Someday	Today
Bored	Energized
Follower	Leader

In other words, when it comes to Outperformers, *Consider. It. Done.* A simple shift in mindset makes all the difference between being good enough and being your best.

To have an Outperforming mindset, two things are required:

First, it starts with desire. Desire gets you going. It is the first spark that starts the burning fire. No great accomplishments happen without the initial desire. It propels you to action.

But desire can also fluctuate from time to time. Think about it – do you *always* have a desire to train? To eat well? To work on your business? To contribute? Aren't there times when, even though you know it's the right thing to do, you just don't want to do it?

The second aspect to an outperforming mindset is commitment. Commitment gets things done, even when it's hard and you're unmotivated. It means that when you sign up for something, you finish it. You make a promise, you honor that promise. You say something will get done; it gets done. It doesn't matter how many storms blow through, you never once question whether coming to the island was the right decision. You've made an unwavering commitment.

Outperform: *Desire + Commitment = You, Unstoppable.*

Training for marathons and Ironmans teaches you a lot about life. It's a great metaphor. Just like one sale doesn't build a business, one workout doesn't make you fit. Rome wasn't built in a day...but it was built *daily*. It's this consistent commitment that all great endurance athletes have.

Training in Minnesota is not easy. Spring can be ugly and brown. Summer can be hot and humid. Fall is beautiful. But by the time most athletes get to Fall, they're tired from training all season long. It's during this time that desire wears off. What seemed like a good idea in May no longer feels like a good idea in September. It's the residual physical and mental fatigue that comes with training over a long period of time (any athlete knows what I'm talking about). I affectionately refer to it as "walking death."

I can always tell which athletes are committed during this time. Uncommitted ones start making excuses and stop showing up. They're too tired, or they had something come up at work, or they "think they just need a day off," or they'll train later on in the day (no, they won't), or they forgot to set their alarm (no, they didn't), or, my favorite, they've found their "peak physical shape" (no, they haven't).

Their desire has just worn off.

A striking contrast to this is, Amy, one of my most dedicated long-term running clients. I swear, if I asked her to, she would run 20 miles every day. It doesn't matter if it's in the dead of Minnesota winter, sub-zero temperatures, alone and at 4:30am, when I ask her to do something, I can *Consider. It. Done.* And because of this, when she tells me that she'll train later in the day (yes, she will) or she had something come up at work, I know it's for real. The committed Outperformers do not make excuses.

The fundamental starting point for high performance is your mindset. High performers THINK differently. Whereas most people see obstacles, they see opportunities. The *"what ifs"* that The Norm experience simply don't exist for Outperformers. And, like all high achievers, when a decision is made that is so strong you know there's NO WAY you'll turn back, it's a game changer. Combine this with a "can do, will do" mindset and committed discipline and you will accomplish just about anything.

The Price of Admission

I'm sitting down for lunch with a new potential client. After we make the typical Minnesotan polite small talk, we get down to business.

"Scott, I really want to lose weight and get into shape."

Wow. I've heard that one once or twice before.

"Okay, two questions: how much weight do you want to lose and what do you mean 'get into shape?' ROUND is a shape, after all."

"Well, I'd like to lose about 20 pounds."

"When is the last time you weighed 20 pounds less than you do right now?"

I secretly fear his response.

"Probably high school."

Saw that one coming from a mile away.

*"That may be **slightly** unrealistic, but we'll come back to it. What about getting into shape?"*

"Not really sure. I would like to gain some muscle and just feel fit."

"How much muscle? Can you define 'feeling fit?'"

"I guess I don't know."

"Ok, no biggie. We'll come back to it later. When do you want to do this by?"

"Summer, preferably."

Sounds like a man with a laser focus, doesn't it?

"Can you be a little more specific? June? July? August?"

"Yeah, I guess any of those would be fine."

Waitress, please bring our food. FAST.

Believe it or not, these meetings are relatively common. He doesn't know what he wants (and what he does want is probably unrealistic), when he wants it and how he's going to get there...which makes it awfully difficult to measure and track progress. Plus, how in the heck do you know if you've arrived at your destination?

I don't condemn people for not knowing the answers to these questions – I simply work with them to clarify, as much as possible, what it is they want. Then, I move into Phase 2: mapping out the *Price of Admission.*

Outperform: *Everything in life has a price of admission tied to it.*

Back to the story...

Based on the lack of a definitive time frame, summer is anywhere from 2-4 months away.

"To start, you're going to need to work out 5 times a week."

"I can't afford to belong to a health club."

Usually this is an excuse.

"What about doing a body-weight based program at home?"

"It's really hard for me to get motivated at home."

Definitely an excuse.

"You're going to need to clean up your diet too. You can start by eating a solid breakfast."

"It's tough for me to wake up earlier in the morning to cook breakfast."

More excuses.

"You'll need to drink a ton of water too. Minimum of 100 ounces a day."

"I don't really like the taste of water. Can I have soda instead?"

Check, please. I'm DONE.

The Price of Admission is a critical part of your mindset. If you want to achieve something great in your life, do you KNOW what it will take to make it happen? Every goal has a price of admission attached to it.

Think of the Price of Admission as currency. When you walk into a store, you can see on the price tag what a product costs. Nothing is hidden. The price tag of an item is a representation of its value. More valuable things command a higher price.

The price of admission for anything you want to accomplish is sometimes less obvious, but no less important. The currency, in this case, is your discipline, dedication, sacrifices, mindset, energy and resourcefulness (just to name a few).

Outperform: *You can accomplish ANYTHING once you know the Price of Admission.*

Here's your simple "Accomplishing Anything" 4-step formula:

Step 1 – Get crystal clear on what you want
Step 2 – Determine the Price of Admission
Step 3 – Ask yourself whether you're willing to pay it?
Step 4 – Revise Step 1 or get to work

I'm very open and honest with my clients when they tell me they want to accomplish something. You tell me what you want and I'll tell you what it takes to get there.

I've coached endurance athletes across hundreds of finish lines and when someone comes to me saying they want to do an Ironman, the first thing I ask them is whether they're ready for a part time job. They always look at me funny...but THAT is the Price of Admission for Ironman training. You'll be swimming, biking and running 15-20 hours per week when you're at the highest training volume.

I'm equally blunt when someone tells me they want to lose enough belly fat to see their abs. Great goal. Lofty, but great. And the Price of Admission attached to being lean enough to see your abs is exercising 6 days per week, drinking a ton of water, eating 5-6 times per day, minimizing alcohol consumption, avoiding significant carbs and fats in the same meal (yes, almost all desserts), planning what you'll eat throughout the course of the day and increasing your protein and vegetable intake.

Outperform: *Great accomplishments require knowing what you'll have to give up to get it.*

Much of the Price of Admission revolves around one simple thing: *sacrifices.*

For anyone wanting to have a successful business, are you willing to be the first one there in the morning and the last one to leave at night? Will you take the time to build a cutting edge product? Will you train your people to be their best? Will you implement the processes to make the business maximally efficient? Will you clean up the messes and put out the fires? Can you deal with the stress at night of knowing it all falls on your shoulders?

I bet new Ironman clients that they'll cry at least three times throughout the course of their training. Again, they look at me funny and don't believe me...but it almost always happens. And I don't care if it challenges my man card – I've cried on the bike more times than I can count. Usually, it happens on a 100-mile bike ride when I'm 50 miles from home – hot, tired and hungry and I realize that the entire way back I'm going to be riding into the wind. Trust me, you feel VERY vulnerable and alone out there.

Nobody else sees this...but behind closed doors, this is the Price of Admission all Ironman triathletes have paid. Unless you've done it, you have no idea that this is the Price of Admission. It is why people are so emotional when they cross the finish line (I'm usually a sobbing mess). It's the culmination of a lot of discipline, dedication and sacrifices. Successful business owners and those with 6-pack abs have paid a similar price. They know what they've done when no one else was watching.

ANYONE who has accomplished great things has paid this price.

I want to emphasize that not wanting to pay the Price of Admission is ok...so long as you're honest with yourself. You're better off sizing up the Price of Admission, admitting you're not willing to pay it, revising your goal to a more realistic one and accomplishing it, than you are to fall short of goal that you were set up to fail at in the first place because you weren't realistic about what you were willing to do and what you were willing to give up. All this is going to do is make you frustrated and feel like a failure.

You may also be saying, "but I don't know what the Price of Admission is for what I want to accomplish." That's fine. I had no idea what my Price of Admission was when I started my own business. In retrospect, it's probably a good thing...because if I would have known how big of a struggle it would be, I may not have done it. I also had no idea how to complete my first Ironman (remember – I had never done a triathlon before!). It was totally foreign to me.

If you don't know the Price of Admission for something, find someone who has done what you want to do and ask them what it will take. Be resourceful. Tell them to give it to you straight and be brutally honest. The Price of Admission is not to be sugar coated. They'll probably also share some strategies they've learned to help you save time.

All high performers share these key character traits – they know what they want, they know the Price of Admission to get it and, most importantly, they are willing to PAY it. They embrace the discipline, dedication and sacrifices required to achieve success. They are necessary components in the process of outperforming.

Fear

When I registered for my first Ironman I was terrified. I remember it like it was yesterday - I was sitting at the computer in the Personal Trainer's "office" at the first health club I worked at. I didn't know what the heck I was doing even being on the website...let alone considering *registering*. At the time, I could barely swim, didn't own a bike and had grown up only running if someone was chasing me.

As I scrolled through the long liability waiver of signing my life away prior to hitting the submit button, it was painfully obvious how afraid I was. I was shaking.

What if I don't finish?

What will people think of me if I don't finish?

What if I crash on the bike?

What if I drown on the swim? (seriously, this was legitimate)

What if I get injured?

What if I'm not CAPABLE?

This last one is the most important. I didn't know if I was good enough. I didn't know if I was worthy.

Outperform: *To do something you've never done, you better bring something you've never brought.*

For many people, they're fearful of whether they can bring something they've never brought. It is classic of the way many of us handle fear, because admitting fear is not an easy thing to do…for any of us. But fear is a very basic survival mechanism when we *perceive* danger or a threat. Still, this *perception* keeps us from growing, from taking risks, from putting ourselves out there and from achieving great things.

WHY does this happen? Simple…

Fear = "What if [insert negative statement]"

When I was very young, my parents took a vacation to the Bahamas, and even though I got to talk to them multiple times when they were gone, I was too young to realize what was going on. I was convinced they had left and were never coming back. Consequently, I developed a horrible stutter and spent years in speech therapy. And for years (like most Americans), I had a huge fear of public speaking. I was afraid I would start stuttering, people would judge me, laugh at me and I would look stupid.

Thankfully, I got over it and now my passion in life is to speak in front of groups. I'm not worried "what if" I start stuttering, or people judge me, laugh at me or I look stupid.

You can overcome ANY fear in your life by doing this ONE SIMPLE THING…

Fearlessness = "What if [insert positive statement]"

What if I hit this submit button, register for Ironman, train flawlessly, execute a perfect race and it ends up being one of the greatest experiences of my life?

This did happen, by the way. But why don't we think like this ALL the time, in ALL situations?

Outperform: *Fear is a Conditioned Response.*

Think about it – what were you afraid of when you were a kid? I used to wake up early on Saturday mornings, lie in bed and patiently wait for my brother to wake up so we could go downstairs to watch cartoons. I hated going downstairs alone. It was dark and scary down there.

But other than this, I didn't fear much, and I'm guessing, you didn't either. And think about the things you fear now – failing, not being good enough, rejection, being alone, having others judge you, going broke, the uncertainty of the future, etc. Were you fearful of these things all your life or are they CONDITIONED RESPONSES based on your personal experiences and societal stimuli?

What is a trait of ALL successful people?
Confidence.

What's the quickest way to build confidence?
Accomplish something great.

What does it take to accomplish something great?
Overcome your fears.

What does it take to overcome your fears? Two things...

First, you can climb into the ring and fight fear head on. You vs. fear and whoever hits the hardest; wins. This can be a great strategy...if you have a "pit bull" type of personality. Someone who is hard charging, competitive and doesn't shy away from confrontation. For some fears, attacking it head on is the ONLY way.

But trying to beat fear into submission also requires a lot of energy. In graduate school I worked with a high level amateur golfer. For many years he was one of the top players at the club. But, unfortunately, he had stunk it up in a few key tournaments and now his confidence was shot. He would get the club to the top of his backswing and BOOM – he would freeze up, unable to hit the ball. He would back off, clear his head and try again. Same thing. After doing this a few times he would usually be able to complete a half-assed full swing...but the results were at a fraction of the level he was used to playing. It was painful to watch and even more painful for him to experience.

The problem? Fear, which was completely based on a negative potential outcome of each shot. He was so worried about hooking, slicing, skulling, duffing, shanking, etc. (all highly technical golf terms) that he couldn't pull the trigger. And what makes golf so mentally challenging is that you spend less than 1% of any given round actually *swinging* the club. All that other time is spent creating either fear or fearlessness in your own head.

So, we started out on the driving range where you're not penalized for the consequence of any shot. This was relatively harmless. Every time we would go onto the golf course, though, I could see the fear and feel the energy being expended. But, in this case, facing the fear on the golf course was the only option. Sometimes getting thrown into the ring with fear and having to fend for yourself is the only way.

It was a long, grueling fight, but thankfully, he overcame his fear and got his game back. By the time we were done he was back to his old self and was once again one of the top players at the club.

Other examples of battling fear this way are people who have post-traumatic stress from an event. It could be someone who was in a horrible car accident getting back into the driver's seat. Or someone who had a devastating relationship trying to love again. Or someone who had a panic attack putting themselves back into a stressful situation. Or someone who tanked a business presentation getting thrown back in with the wolves.

Encountering your fear is NEVER easy...but there's no use standing on the outside. Get into the ring! That's where the magic happens and you find out what's deep inside. Once you're in the ring you'll find that fear isn't so tough after all. It gets better, and easier, with time.

Second, you can have a belief and a purpose so strong that fear squashes in comparison. This is faith, and not totally in the spiritual sense. It's faith in yourself, what you're doing and what you're capable of. When these are strong, fear doesn't stand a chance.

Outperform: *Accomplishing Anything = Faith > Fear*

The majority of very successful athletes have this type of faith. They believe in themselves (or something greater than themselves) so wholeheartedly that fear isn't even on their radar. When the pressure is the greatest, they are at their best. It's almost an eerie sense of calm as they let it happen instead of trying to force it. They were born for this. Everything always works out.

Successful business leaders are no different. When everyone else is shaking and scrambling, they're a rock. Their self-belief is such that they'll put the whole company on their back and not shrink from any perceived negative outcome. They're not afraid to take risks and they can always find a positive way out of any situation.

If you want to succeed in the Accomplish Anything formula, you either have to increase faith or decrease fear. The bulk of increasing faith comes from stacking accomplishments (even minor ones). You've done it before and you can do it again.

The key question to ask to decrease fear is: *what's the worst that can happen?* Americans usually rank public speaking as their most feared thing, with death as a close second. So, really, what's the WORST that can happen? Is what you fear going to cause you to DIE?

If I would have been thinking rationally while registering for Ironman I would have realized that, even if I couldn't swim, I knew how to tread water, and thus, I probably wasn't going to DIE on the swim. Not sure this would have stopped me from shaking but having this realization would have, at least, decreased my fear.

Many people use FEAR as an acronym of False Evidence Appearing Real. Because it is. Consider the following stats:

- 40% of things we fear would never happen (the world will end, global flooding)
- 30% of things we fear happened in the past
- 10% of things we fear are insignificant
- 12% of things we fear are health issues that will not happen

This means 92% of the things we fear WILL NEVER HAPPEN.

So, whatever you fear is likely not going to happen in the first place. If it does, *seriously*, what's the worst thing that can happen? Someone will reject you? You can handle it. Someone will judge you? That says more about them than you. Failing? It's only a failure if you don't learn something from it. Being alone? You have plenty of people who care about you. You'll go broke? Probably won't happen...you'll figure a way out. An uncertain future? The future is always uncertain...but today's a gift – that's why they call it The Present.

It's a simple shift of focus.

I'm convinced that, if we are not doing something that we genuinely want to do, fear is always holding us back on some level. Be careful of who you surround yourself with, too. If someone isn't able to do something, they'll tell you that you can't either. And we're dumb enough to believe them. We're dumb enough to believe society. We live in fear that we're not capable either. Shame on us for letting others steal our dreams.

Don't live your life paralyzed by fear. Live it driven by desire.

MASTER THE
FUNDAMENTALS

No Weaknesses

Fundamentals are the basic building blocks of anything in life. They are the foundation of the house. When the foundation of the house is solid and strong, you can build a higher ceiling because it has a better base of support.

Without first developing the fundamentals, you're treading on a slippery slope. You try to continue building a higher ceiling without a strong foundation and the house is going to collapse...especially when it is pushed, tested and put under pressure.

What are the fundamentals of good basketball players? Most would say dribbling, scoring, free throws, passing, rebounding, and playing defense. You master these and you'll be tough to beat on the basketball court.

Growing up, my favorite basketball player was Michael Jordan. Yes, I was *that kid* who had posters of him hanging in my bedroom (they're actually still there) and I would cut out articles in magazines and the newspaper and put those up too. I had all his videos and I would watch every game I could.

Most experts agree that Jordan was the greatest scorer (if not the greatest player) who ever lived. But many people fail to realize he was on the NBA All-Defensive first team nine times (tied for most ever) and was an 80%+ career free throw shooter for his career (very good). He was also an above average rebounder and passer.

In other words, he had no weaknesses, which is another way of saying he had mastered the fundamentals. You could not expose him. I'll be the first to say, what made Jordan the best ever was his mindset (and this is the reason Mindset comes before Fundamentals in this book). He was hyper-competitive, believed in himself and had the desire to beat you at all costs. This was a necessary prerequisite and is why, when you layer mastery of the fundamentals on top of this (and athleticism to boot), you have the greatest player ever.

Contrast this with many NBA Centers who cannot shoot free throws. Sure, they're great for defense, scoring and rebounding, but they're a liability late in games. When they are tested and put under pressure, they get EXPOSED. The same can be said for *any* player at *any* position with *any* weakness. Eventually, it will come back to hurt them, and usually at the least opportune times. The fundamentals matter most in the biggest moments. This is why, the brighter the spotlight shined on Jordan in the playoffs, the better he played.

Outperform: *Everything in life has basic fundamentals that are REQUIRED for success.*

Consider...

Health fundamentals: nutrition, hydration, sleep, stress and exercise.

Business fundamentals: sales, marketing, innovation, manufacturing, distribution, and employee development.

Relationship fundamentals: love, trust, intimacy, commitment, honesty, compromise and understanding.

If you're not performing as well as you'd like to in any area of your life, you're weak in the fundamentals. Period. Strengthen them and you'll perform better. Doing this virtually guarantees you'll have success. You will have built a foundation that stands the test of time.

Outperform: *Regardless of how long you've been doing something, go back to the fundamentals to continue to improve.*

When I was in graduate school, I had an assistantship teaching golf classes to undergraduates. The classes were offered at three separate levels – beginner, intermediate and advanced. Many of the beginners had never touched a club before, whereas some of those in the advanced course were single digit handicappers (very good). But I started them ALL by looking at the same 4 things:

Grip – Stance – Alignment – Posture

Now, some of the advanced players could not believe these were the first things being taught. They thought I'd immediately jump into advanced techniques of swing angles, paths and planes. But here's the rational: regardless of your ability level, golf is played from a *static* position. And if you're not perfectly positioned when you're getting ready to hit the ball, what chances do you have of being successful once the swing starts? If you start the swing from a faulty position, you're going to *have to* make compensatory movements to hit a good shot. There's no other way.

When I was a regional sales manager for a global technology company, I constantly had decisions to make when determining how I would reach my quota. If I was behind in my numbers, I would either need to market more (reach more people), sell more (convert a higher % of prospects) or know my product better. These were the three fundamentals I was in charge of as a sales manager. If I didn't know my product, I'd have to sell and market a helluva lot to make my quota. Or conversely, maybe I knew my product well and had a very high sales conversion rate but I wasn't marketing to reach enough people. Either of these signifies having to make compensatory movements because you're starting from a faulty position.

Outperform: *The little things amount to the BIGGEST things.*

Fundamentals are a way to make complex things seem very simple. It's very easy for us to get daunted when lofty goals are put in front of us. We start to panic, looking at everything required to get the job done. But fundamentals allow you to break down *any* goal into its most basic form. By focusing on the fundamentals with the proper mindset and commitment, you'll eventually get to any goal you have.

"Blocking" or "Chunking" Your Time

Think about when you were in school. For many, this will be the most efficient time in your life for learning and applying knowledge. And it had less to do with your brain being in a time that was ripe for learning. It had everything to do with the way you blocked your time.

When you were in school, you had a set period of time that you would learn about one subject. You would learn, review, apply, collaborate and be tested on ONE thing. And because you knew there was a precisely defined period of time for you to study something, you got a lot more out of it. You were fully immersed.

Why don't you approach your productivity this same way?

What if you said you were only going to work from 8-5 with no exceptions (some people do this quite successfully)? The initial fear for most Outperformers is that, if you've been putting in 10-12 hour days up to this point, there's no way everything is going to get done. And you may be right...but give it a shot. What you'll come to realize is that you are much more efficient and effective with your time. More gets done, faster, when you're put on the clock. Your focus goes to another level.

Outperform: *You cannot make diamonds without pressure. Embrace it.*

Didn't you ever have to write a paper the night before it was due? Were you not HIGHLY productive when you were under the gun and you really needed to be?

I was the king of staying up all night to write a paper that was due the next day. I'm not saying this is the most practical strategy for writing effectively but for the most part, it worked pretty well. Every paper I ever had to write got done...and the grades were satisfactory. But there was *something* about my personality that struggled to get going on something until I was really put under pressure to do it. I needed a firm deadline. Something that scared me a little bit.

So, when you're approaching your day, decide what fundamentals are most important, block time for them and *attach deadlines*. No more than 90 minutes can be blocked at a time, because remember, when the body turns off, the brain turns off. And you want to make sure you stay maximally sharp with what you're doing. Plowing through hours in a zombie-like state is probably not much better than what you may be doing right now. And make sure your attached deadline creates enough pressure to *make you* move forward in a focused, productive way.

Advanced Training: The Sub-fundamentals

We just got done talking about school, so let's start with the basic fundamentals of math:

Addition – Subtraction – Multiplication – Division

If you can't do these four things, you can't do math. Everything else is a sub-fundamental of these basic things. Unless you have learned, and mastered, these basic fundamentals FIRST, it's pointless to go on to geometry, calculus, trigonometry, etc.

Outperform: *Without the fundamentals, it's useless to work on anything else.*

Once you have achieved mastery of the fundamentals, each of them can be broken down into sub-fundamentals. To go back to basketball, shooting can be broken down into foot placement, leg bend, hand position, elbow angle, follow through, etc. The basic fundamentals alone make you tough to beat – perfecting the little things make you UNSTOPPABLE.

I've been to all types of sales seminars. Find the prospect's pain, build trust with them, ask for the sale, create a need, differentiate your product, leverage the competition, create fear, and emphasize benefits rather than features. Depending on whose sales philosophy you follow, each of these could be things that would contribute to you being better in the fundamental of sales conversion.

The best business leaders in the world know their numbers and operations...backwards and forwards...in every division and department. Their attention to detail is what got them to where they are. And this attention to detail is also what's necessary to have an outperforming business.

A good question to ask – if I'm weak in one fundamental, what are the little things I need to improve to become better in this area? If sales are low (a fundamental), what are the sub-fundamentals (sales training, product differentiation, knowing your competition) that would improve this area? Then, block time based on these specific things that need to be improved upon.

Sub-fundamentals are the specific skills, processes and procedures necessary to perform a fundamental well. All you have to do to determine your sub-fundamentals is to ask yourself the following question:

Which one area do I want to improve and WHAT will it take to make that happen?

The one area is the fundamental and the *"what"* are the sub-fundamentals.

Yes, it really is THAT simple. Fundamentals, sub-fundamentals and blocking time. Do it and you'll improve your productivity and results exponentially.

If you're not spending at least half of your time developing the fundamentals, you're missing the boat. You're flirting with being all flash and no substance. Beware of being exposed. But by investing your time on the basic building blocks of your house, you will be able to raise your performance ceiling that much higher. And regardless of whether it is tested, pressured or hit with stormy weather, it will stand the test of time.

Focused Productivity

Productivity is your ability to get things DONE.

We are all investment managers of our time. We start out with the same finite amount of time – 24 hours in a day, 168 hours in a week. But just like our own individual portfolios, some invest well and some invest poorly.

Outperform: *Productive people have the best investment strategies.*

Really, that's all it boils down to – successful people have found a way to get more done in the same amount of time. They're damn smart investors. And if you want to make your mark in your time here on earth, you better focus your productivity to maximize the people you impact.

Behold the top 12 strategies Outperformers use for focused productivity:

1. Be grateful

Every single day, when you wake up, you should be grateful for what you have and what you've been given. This includes your relationships, gifts, talents, skills, possessions, abilities, health, happiness and *current* circumstances (no matter what they are).

There have been sport psychology studies done on the highest performing athletes and one of the traits they display is an extreme level of gratefulness and gratitude on a daily basis. "Easy," you may say, "they're top performing athletes. OF COURSE there's a lot to be grateful for!" But has it ever occurred to you that part of what allowed them to become a top performer was their level of gratitude?

The distinction is that, rather than focus on what they don't have and the things missing in their life, they concentrate on the positives of what they're going to do with them. And because of this, they are always working from an empowered mindset that drives them to not only be appreciative of their current situation but also have a desire to contribute and improve upon it.

There's a cardiologist who lives in my condo complex. Roughly 50 years young. Up until about 6 months ago, he was a very high functioning individual. Unfortunately, he suffered a massive stroke and is now confined to a wheelchair. I see him almost daily. He always has a smile on his face (part of it is that he loves my dog!) but as I see his caretakers helping him in and out of the car, through the doorways and elevators, I'm constantly reminded to be grateful for my own level of health. And every time I want to bitch and whine about being tired and not "feeling like" doing something, namely working, training or simply walking my dog, I realize that there are many others who are not as fortunate. I need to quit complaining, get over myself and be grateful for what I have.

2. Meditate and get focused in the morning

Slowing down and taking time to *relax* is one of the most difficult things for Type-A, driven overachievers. But that's exactly what I'm talking about with meditation and focus.

Outperform: *Slowing down your mind will speed up your productivity.*

Just to clarify, I'm not talking about anything voodoo with meditation. Yes, when you properly meditate your brain waves change and it allows your brain a "break" from the constant chaos of everyday life...but I'm not talking about being "one with the earth" and harnessing its plentiful energy. Way too weird for me. I need concrete.

Analyze great athletes before competition and you'll likely see them listening to music, eyes closed, getting focused on what they're about to do. They do this to get centered, in a place where they're calm, their brain turns off and they're poised for peak performance. Because this is their livelihood, they know any amount of stress, lack of preparation or mental errors will cost them.

Why don't we approach our days with this level of focused energy? Instead, we wake up and are literally "shot out of a cannon." We jump out of bed, don't nourish our bodies, and immediately check our email or social media profiles. Then, before we know it, we're bombarded with so many tasks that we spend our days completely reactive...instead of proactive and creative. We never took a few minutes to slow down, get mentally prepared and ready for what we wanted to accomplish.

3. Make a to do list...and accept not doing all of it

I've tried every way of creating to-do lists that you can imagine. Notebooks, post-it notes, special template paper, apps on my phone, outlook, etc., and I have finally settled on one that has worked for me:

Notecards.

Yes, simple notecards like you used back in elementary school. Part of what has made it so successful has been that I can only fit a few things on a single notecard (and I only use one side) that I'm going to accomplish each day. It saves me from myself...where I used to write down 50 things I was going to do in a day and it was tough to even get started because I didn't know where to begin. This keeps it simple and manageable.

Interestingly enough, though, even when using notecards, I barely ever accomplish everything I write down. And at first, I would get down on myself because of it. *Why can't you get it all done, Scott?!? Why are you so pathetically unproductive?!?*

Since, I've eased up on myself a bit and put things in perspective. Even if the list isn't 100% completed, isn't it still MUCH better than doing nothing at all? Forward progress has been made. I may not be at the finish line but I'm closer to it than when I started.

4. Tackle the most challenging tasks before lunch (when you have your most energy)

You have your most energy in the morning. It's true for everyone...regardless of whether you consider yourself a "morning person" (I certainly am not). Why? You have just completed your greatest source of energy renewal: sleep. And, even if you have a few cobwebs in the morning and it takes you some time to wake up, you have your most energy at this time.

So tackle your tasks that require the most energy when you have the most energy to devote to it (the morning). Doing this ensures you'll have the juice to complete the tasks.

The next step is identifying which tasks are the most challenging for you...and are also the most important for moving your health, happiness or high performance, to the next level.

Perhaps you hate to work out but it's easy for you to eat well. *Work out in the morning.*

Maybe you hate to do sales calls but it's easy for you to do product research. *Make your sales calls in the morning.*

Or you hate to do laundry but it's easy for you to do everything but laundry. *Fine - I will start doing my laundry in the morning!*

Outperform: *Accomplishments in the morning = juice for the afternoon.*

Completing your most challenging tasks before lunch gives you a twofold effect – you've already accomplished something significant early in the day and it empowers you with momentum to accomplish even more in the afternoon.

Consider the flip side of this where you do everything that's easy in the morning and put off the things that are hard until the afternoon...when your energy is already somewhat drained. Then, it's easy to blow off doing the laundry and say you'll do it the next day. But the same thing happens again, and before you know it, you have no clean clothes and you're FORCED to do laundry out of necessity!

I seriously need laundry therapy...but you get my point.

5. Take more breaks

Outperform: *When your body turns off, your brain turns off.*

Your brain has a minimum amount of time to stay engaged. Even the most focused, productive people on the planet need to rest their brains from time to time.

This can be accomplished by efficiently taking breaks. There is no "set" amount of time that a break needs to be. New Balance has done studies that show 1-2 minutes can be beneficial. Others advocate at least 5-10 minutes for a break.

But the most important part of a break is that you get off your duff, move around, clear your head and get the neurons in your brain firing again.

Fresh air can also be a magic cure all. This is especially true if almost all your time is spent at a desk, in meeting rooms or in seminars. Fresh air gives you more oxygen to breathe, which facilitates mental alertness and cognitive capacity. And it can be as short as walking around outside for 1-2 minutes.

When Tiger Woods plays golf, any given round will take 4-5 hours. And, for even one of the most mentally strong athletes on the planet, you need to take breaks. You need to come out of your "zone." That's what golf is – a series of entering in and breaking out of the zone. Tennis is no different. If you tried to concentrate the entire time, your level of productivity would eventually start to decrease because the neurons wouldn't be firing as acutely as they once were.

Please think about this the next time you're sitting at your desk for multiple hours at a time without a break.

6. Minimize distractions

There are distractions all around us. Distractions can be people, technology or even our own self-imposed barriers.

What qualifies as a distraction? Anything that does not take you closer to what you want to accomplish.

I love telling the following joke, usually in the summer:

"Did you know that Minnesota only has two seasons?"

The person always looks at me, puzzled...

"Yes, it's true. Winter and road construction."

Outperform: *Distractions are self-imposed road construction. Get rid of it and you'll get to your destination faster.*

Look at this in two ways. Let's take bad reality TV, for example. If you've been maximally productive throughout the week, made all the progress you want to and bad reality TV is a way for you to de-stress and unwind after a long week, that could be seen as a strategic "break," or source of energy renewal. However, if watching bad reality TV is a method of wasting time that is taking away from what you really *should be* doing to accomplish your goals, it is a distraction. And you need to get rid of it.

These days, by far the biggest sources of distraction are technology related. It's great that you can connect with anyone, anywhere in the world, at a moment's notice. But not being able to unplug from this and focus on what truly needs to get done can also be a huge distraction. How many times do you stop in the middle of what you're doing to check social media, email, send a text or answer the phone? And are any of these really that URGENT? *Any* one of these is a distraction from the primary objective. Can you imagine how much more productive you'd be if you could just have a singular productive focus?

7. Use technology with intent and STOP multitasking

When you sit down at the computer to do something, know EXACTLY what it is you're going to do. If you sit down at the computer without any formal plan of what you're going to accomplish, you'll end up wasting time. It's waaaay too easy to get caught up checking email, social media, playing games or surfing the web.

It's important to separate using technology as a tool for focused productivity vs. using it for entertainment. The two should never crisscross...and if you're using technology with a specific intention, they won't. You'll know when you're sitting down at the computer for the purpose of getting things done and you'll know when you're sitting down at the computer for fun and leisure. Doing this will not only increase your productivity but it will probably help you relax and enjoy it that much more when you're sitting down to have fun.

Outperform: *Never mix using the computer for fun and leisure with using the computer for focused productivity. Separate them.*

There is also a common misconception that the most successful people are excellent multi-taskers. They're not. Neurological studies have shown that the brain is incapable of multi-tasking. It's only capable of focusing on one thing at a time.

The most productive people are extremely efficient at accomplishing tasks and they're able to swiftly move from task to task, with little time needed to "regroup." Improving this skill allows them to handle a variety of tasks in many different areas and adapt to almost any unique situation.

8. Practice deep breathing

Simple exercise for you:

First, close your eyes and imagine you're nervous and ridden with anxiety. You can't focus on one thing because you have so many thoughts swirling around in your head. How are you breathing?

Second, close your eyes and imagine you're totally relaxed and confident. You can accomplish anything because you know exactly what you're doing. How are you breathing?

Breathing is an involuntary action that we do everyday...but HOW we do it has a massive impact on our productivity, mood and mindset. Short, fast and shallow breaths mean you're nervous and tense. Long, slow and deep breaths mean you're relaxed and poised.

The Norm: *Short, fast and shallow breathing.*

Outperform: *Long, slow and deep breathing.*

The stress of our day-to-day lives causes changes in our breathing patterns. We're never going to STOP breathing (or not anytime soon, hopefully)...but we will alter the way in which we do it. At any given time, however, if you focus on deep breathing, it will automatically return you to a more self-assured, productive mindset.

9. Improve email and social media systems

In the 21ˢᵗ century, email and social media have superseded the idiot box as the biggest time wasters for people. I'll deal with it in two parts:

First, email. One of my longtime mentors, Brendon Burchard, calls email "a convenient organizing system for other people's agendas." He's 100% correct...based on the way most people use email.

There are a couple of simple ways to determine if this is you. When you sit down at your computer or when you open email on your phone, what's the *specific* purpose for you doing that? In other words, are you doing it to CHECK email or to SEND email? If it's the former, is there something in particular you're checking for...or are you just going to check whatever comes in? If you're responding to whatever comes in, you're living in a reactive email mode based on whatever gets thrown at you...which is the way most people approach email.

Stats on social media are even more alarming. People spend, on average 2-3 hours PER DAY on social media (you *really* don't have time to exercise?). That's 14-21 hours per week. Do this for an entire year and you will have spent over 30 DAYS on social media. What could you accomplish if you had 30 extra days and you weren't taking pictures of your food or your cat accidentally jumping in the dishwasher?

Outperform: *Go ahead and eat your food. We don't need to see a picture of it on Facebook.*

Also consider the following simple stats:

- Those with low household income spend significantly more time on social media than those with high household incomes.
- Those with low education levels spend significantly more time on social media than those with high education levels.
- Unemployed spend significantly more time on social media than those who are employed.

Which category are you in? Which category do you *want* to be in? Enough said.

10. Stay inspired

Inspiration comes from within. And staying inspired is connected to the deeper purpose of why you're doing something. Unlike motivation that can flee from moment to moment (discussed later), inspiration is that fire burning deep in the pit of your belly. It never dies out.

Inspiration never leaves us but it can get clouded from time to time. But all that's necessary is to bring back a cue to trigger it to the forefront.

My top 4 ways to stay inspired:

I. Read: Read something that moves you. Something that strikes a chord in you, like the author is speaking DIRECTLY to you (maybe this book?). I love reading inspiring quotes.

II. Pictures: Look at pictures that are meaningful to you. Many of my favorites are pictures with family and friends...and some of my accomplishments (like crossing the finish line in Ironman).

III. Music: We ALL have songs that fire us up, no matter what mood we're currently in. Whatever these songs are, they are your secret weapons. Use them.

IV. Video: With modern technology, watching videos has never been easier. And the bonus to videos is that it is the only one that hits two senses: visual (seeing) and auditory (hearing). These two things can often make videos *the most* inspirational of all. Just think of all those movies that made you cry!

Whichever one of these you select, make sure it triggers an *emotion* inside of you. If it doesn't, find something that will. But I'm betting every single person reading this book has a few quotes, pictures, songs or videos that they know will stir the inspirational pot. The only trick is to bring these out when you feel your productivity starting to slide.

11. Learn how to say no

"People pleasers" – this one is for you.

Learning to say no is difficult. We think that, by saying no, we're being selfish. To me, there's nothing selfish about saying no – it simply means we're clear on what we want and we're willing to say no if it doesn't fit in our plan of getting there.

A friend of mine is a self-employed online marketer and a prolific writer. And like many writers, he keeps a tight schedule. Every weekday morning at 9am, he is writing. It doesn't matter if it's a blog post or a new book.

And sometimes I'll ask him if he wants to grab a coffee in the morning and chat. He ALWAYS says no, even though I know darn well there is nothing else on his schedule. He doesn't have any kids and he could write at any point in the day.

But that's not the point – he KNOWS what he wants to accomplish and knows what he needs to do to maximize his productivity. He won't be as efficient writing in the afternoon or evening as he is at 9am. And because of this, anything that comes up during this time, he says no to.

As much as it infuriates me to have him say no – I respect his routine and his level of focused productivity. Pay close attention to what decisions you're making that are interrupting your productive patterns and don't be afraid to say no if it isn't bringing you closer to where you want to go.

Outperform: *No doesn't always mean "no." Sometimes it means "not now."*

12. Set timelines

I was a slacker in college. I did the minimal amount of work to get by for my first 3.5 years. I could only cram for a test if I knew it was coming up. I could only *truly* write a paper when I knew it was due the next day. And I could only complete a project if I was working on it until the last possible minute.

Was I a slacker? Yes. Procrastinator? Yes. Did I benefit *greatly* from timelines? YES!

Everyone benefits from timelines and you don't have to be like me to make it work for you. Because we all have a natural tendency to focus on what's urgent instead of what's important, if there is something in your life you want to accomplish and you're not doing it, you haven't set a clearly defined timeline on it. Timelines light a fire under your ass and drive you to higher levels of action and productivity.

Outperform: *Timelines commit you to GETTING. IT. DONE.*

Like fundamentals, if you have lofty long-term goals, break them down with sub-timelines. Larger businesses have to work this way. If you have huge growth and expansion goals you must break them down with smaller, more immediate timelines. The same thing goes for people wanting to lose large amounts of weight. Let these serve as "checkpoints" on your way to the finish line.

Focused productivity is nothing more than finding out what works for you and applying it over and over again to achieve results. I seriously doubt anyone reading this book has mastered all 12 of these strategies (nor does anyone necessarily *need* to). If you are using a few of them and they work for you, stick with it. Sometimes less is more.

If you're brand new and you don't know where to begin, pick ONE productivity strategy that you're going to focus on for the next month. Yes, ONE. And do it, consistently, for the entire month. After the month is done, pick another one and focus on it for 30 days. Then pick a third one. Keep doing this until you've reached your peak level of focused productivity. And if you continue employing all 12 strategies over the course of an entire year, I will bet the farm it will be the highest performing year of your *life* – all areas.

DURABILITY

Resilience

In life, one thing is certain—expect the unexpected. Highs and lows. Ups and downs. Triumph and misery. Success and failure. Hope and despair. Comfort and fear. Pleasure and pain. Joy and suffering.

Life is a roller coaster...not a train ride. Accept it. Learn from it. Have fun with it.

These final chapters are about durability. Durability means you will stand the test of time. That, no matter how badly things seem to be breaking down, you'll still be there. You will not shrink and you will not go away. In fact, you will come back even stronger.

> **Outperform:** *When you're durable, you can withstand a good beating from life.*

Durability is a key component for success in health, business, relationships and life. And being durable starts with accepting and embracing adversity. This is the first step towards building resiliency.

I always tell my athletes before a race to *"expect the best but prepare for the worst."* From an endurance athletic perspective, many wish…and hope…and pray…that they'll feel good the whole race. This almost *never* happens and if you set yourself up with the false hope of feeling good start to finish, you don't know what the heck to do if you start to feel bad. I always tell athletes – EXPECT that a race is going to hurt, but EXPECT that you have the confidence, determination and ability to overcome it. Trust in yourself and trust in your training and preparation. Trust in any area of life is no different.

My 2012 Ironman was a prime example of resiliency. I was fit, mentally prepared, motivated (I had a new girlfriend who I REALLY wanted to impress) and I had aspirations of qualifying for the Kona Ironman…which is basically the Superbowl of Ironmans.

When I did my first Ironman Wisconsin (IMWI) six years before, they were capping the field at 2200 athletes. Now they allowed 2800. The IMWI swim turned into the most obnoxious water-based royal rumble I'd ever seen and I almost had a panic attack. There were so many people around me and, regardless of which side I was breathing on, I was swallowing so much water that it got a little scary. But I talked myself down and controlled what I could control…which was basically rumbling forward.

Next up was the bike, where the first 30-40 miles were uneventful. I could tell I didn't have the best legs that day but I knew the course, knew how to make up time, and knew how to pace myself. I figured it would all work out fine.

Then it went bad. Reeeeeeeally bad.

I've never had significant knee pain in my life but at mile 40 I started getting sharp, shooting pain on the outside of my right knee. It was going all the way down my tibia (shin). Initially, the pain was coming and going and I was able to mostly ride through it.

But it kept getting worse. And worse. And worse. And worse.

The sharp pain turned into a massive dull ache. I couldn't push a gear. I got off my bike twice to massage and stretch, but no luck. I tried riding knock-kneed and bow-legged. No luck. I tried shifting my weight forward and back in the saddle. No luck.

I always said I'd never involve God in a triathlon but, on this day, I even tried praying. Still no luck.

Fast forward to mile 105. I've been biking with, more or less, one leg for the last 50+ miles. There are a couple of steep hills on Whalen Rd coming back into Madison and I had to WALK my bike up the last hills. My knee hurt too badly to pedal up it. My head was slumped down and I was crying. A total woe-is-me, why-is-this-happening pity party. I was lower than low.

Outperform: *We ALL throw pity parties. But how long before you suck it up and move on?*

I'd bet the farm that I've never gotten passed in the last 10 miles of an Ironman bike, but on this day, I get passed by at least 50 people. As people flew by, I got many words of encouragement because everyone thought I was just tired. They had no idea.

So, after my 5:48 bike (31 minutes SLOWER than my previous best) I take my sweet time starting the run. At this point, I'm simply wishing that my damned right knee would just numb out so I can at least *hobble* through the marathon and not have to walk the entire thing. 26.2 miles takes a long time to *run*...but I would be out there ALL DAY if I had to *walk* it.

The first mile is brutally slow and I'm basically dragging my right leg behind me. But I can also feel it loosening up and by the time I get into the second mile, I start to think this might be doable after all.

With each stride it becomes apparent that whatever was killing me on the bike is going to be a non-issue on the run, but I still toy with the idea of running really slowly and taking it all in, while minimizing the suffering. And why not? I have nothing to run for. I'm going to miss my goal time by at least 30 minutes. I'm not going to qualify for Kona. I'm not going to impress my new girlfriend.

But that's not my style. When I do something I try to do my best at it and there's nothing I hate more than looking in the mirror after a race knowing I didn't try my best. Trying my best is ALWAYS something I can control.

Shouldn't this be our attitude towards everything in life?

It was then that I decided I HAD TO end that Ironman on a good note. I couldn't go 0-for-3 that day on swimming, biking and running. It would leave such a sick taste of unfinished business in my mouth.

Outperform: *Wasting your potential by not trying your best is criminal.*

Anyone who has done Ironman knows the final marathon is about survival. You simply try to disintegrate as little as possible. I finished the marathon in 3:34, which was my *best* Ironman marathon by 14 minutes. I got beaten down...but I came back stronger.

I will always consider this one of my BEST races because of the sweet satisfaction that came from giving it my all when, with a subpar swim and a disaster of a bike, there was ZERO incentive for me to do so. It would have been so easy to throw in the towel and quit.

To be an Outperformer, you better get comfortable with things not always going your way. Racing is a great metaphor for life (especially races like the previous example). Life is hard and things rarely go according to plan. There can be huge, seemingly never-ending lows. But when this happens, are you going to bitch up and throw yourself a continual pity party or are you going to turn it around and make the best of an unfortunate situation?

The rest of this book is about accepting and embracing the fact that, no matter how healthy you are, how happy you are, how strong of a mindset you have and how well you master the fundamentals, life is still going to smack you around from time to time, out of nowhere and for no apparent reason. And it's better that we get it out on the table now than for you to feel that your life is going to be *endlessly* smooth sailing after reading this book. You need to know how to right the ship when you get knocked off course.

Nietzsche famously said "that which does not kill us makes us stronger." That's why the next two chapters are going to be about adopting specific strategies to bolster resiliency and your response to adversity. Remember, it's not the obstacles in life that matter…it's how you RESPOND to the obstacles that makes all the difference. *That* is durability. *That* is what makes you an Outperformer.

Unshakable Self Confidence

You can't outperform without confidence. It's a necessary component to taking risks, seeking challenges and, most importantly, responding to adversity. Think of *any* successful person you know in *any* area of life – do *any* of them lack confidence? No way, Jose. When life deals you lemons, even if no one else believes in your ability to make lemonade, YOU have to believe it. Confidence is arrogance under control. The only ones bothered by it are the ones who secretly wish they had it too.

I remember sitting down for the interview that would eventually become my last corporate job and the head of HR was giving me the standard grilling (*"tell me about a time when you had to be diplomatic and didn't take no for an answer."*). Ugh. I'd rather be grinding my fingernails on a chalkboard.

Eventually, she asked me...

"Tell me about a time in your life when you failed."

My response: *"I've never failed at anything before."*

Looking back, I can't believe I said this. Not because I don't believe it, but because I *really* wanted to get the job and I'm surprised I didn't give a more "acceptable" answer. I'd give anything to know what she was thinking at that time (it couldn't have been too bad – I got the job).

When she asked me to elaborate, I explained that the only way you can *truly* fail at something is to not learn from it. Otherwise, life is just a series of mistakes and lessons learned, that you use to do better in the future. We're all on a continual course of self-correction. The biggest crime is to continue to make the same mistakes, over and over, and never learn anything. *That* is failure.

For the rest of this chapter, I'll refer to failure in the "traditional" sense, but now you know my opinion on failure.

We've already come to grips with the fact that, sometimes, negative events are going to happen to us. How we EXPLAIN these events, either positive or negative, is called our explanatory style. And it will make or break our durability by shaping the way we respond to our situations and circumstances.

These are the 3 central components to explanatory style:

Permanence - Stable vs. Unstable (when something happens, will it *continue* to happen?).

Pervasiveness - Localized vs. Global (when something happens, will it happen in *other* areas?).

Personalization - Personal vs. External (when something happens, were you responsible? Was it your fault?).

Whether you realize it or not, your explanatory style, based on positive or negative events, shapes your destiny. It determines whether you bounce back stronger and try again or whether you live your life jaded and close-minded.

For example, if The Norm fails at dieting (negative event), here's how they explain it:

"Dieting never works for me. I always fail." (Permanence)

"I can't do anything right. Everything has been going wrong for me lately." (Pervasiveness)

"It was all my fault. I don't have the willpower to do it. I'm such a loser. I suck." (Personalization)

Outperformers explain a failed diet this way:

"Oh well, it didn't work this time. The next time will be different." (Permanence)

"I have plenty of things going right in other areas of my life." (Pervasiveness)

"Maybe this wasn't the right type of diet for me. I can find something else that will work better." (Personalization)

When a positive event occurs (you lose weight, build a business, accomplish something), it's the exact opposite. The Norm *doesn't* think they were responsible ("I was just lucky"), *doesn't* think it'll happen again ("it was a one-shot deal") and *doesn't* think it'll translate to other areas ("that's great, but I still can't do blah blah blah"). Outperformers see it differently.

As you can see, this simple shift in explanatory style has massive consequences on how you see the world and what future opportunities you'll embrace. What you tell yourself on a daily basis *matters*. Big time.

Our explanatory styles can be our own worst enemy. When you fell while learning to walk, why didn't you just say screw it and crawl for the rest of your life? You didn't know what you were doing and you were failing *constantly*...in plain view for others to see. How embarrassing! What has changed? What's different when you fail now?

Outperform: *Embrace a positive explanatory style or crawl for the rest of your life.*

A good exercise is for *all of us* to look at our attitudes and our assumptions towards certain things, whether these are products, people, politics, or anything else. WHY do we have these beliefs? How were they formed? Are they rational or did something so traumatic happen that warped our entire view ever since?

Yes, looking at our explanatory styles and the "lens" with which we see the world requires introspection. It's useful for us to understand how we arrived at where we are...and if this is not where we want to be, it can help in moving us towards where we want to go.

 Total Confidence

*Great audio mp3 in the **Outperformer's Vault** on the science of Total Confidence.*

OutperformTheNorm.com/Vault

One of the biggest misconceptions is that successful people never fail. BS! Successful people fail *all the time*. They fail and fail and fail and fail, and because of this, they succeed.

They never give up...and part of the reason they never give up is because they have explanatory styles that allow them to continue failing without it ruining their confidence and self-image. They're bulletproof to failure.

Let's consider some statistics of the highest performing athletes on the planet.

Jack Nicklaus won 18.9% of the tournaments he played in and many consider him the greatest golfer of all time. This means 81.1% of the time, or more than 4 out of every 5 times he teed it up, *he lost*. Any golfer who loses less than 90% of the time will probably be in the Hall of Fame.

Ted Williams is one of the greatest baseball hitters in history with a career batting average of .344. So, more than 6 out of every 10 times he was at the plate, he either struck out or hit into an out. Any baseball player who fails less than 7 out of every 10 times will likely be in the Hall of Fame.

Roger Federer has won more grand slam tournaments than any male tennis player. His overall winning percentage is 69%. More than 3 out of every 10 times he plays, he loses. And he is only playing against one opponent at a time! Any tennis player who loses less than 4 out of every 10 times will certainly be in the Hall of Fame.

I cite these statistics for two reasons. First, these are the top players in the *history* of their sport. And even when you're the highest of the high performers, you still lose, more than most people realize. Everyone sees the celebrated spotlight of success. We see them on the idiot box. On Sportscenter. On prime time. We see the "after picture"...not the before. Very few recognize or appreciate the failures these athletes had on the way there.

The second thing to realize is that, to become the best there ever was, these players didn't just lose a few times. They had to lose over and over to succeed at a level that eventually made them the best. And even though I cited percentages, Jack Nicklaus lost over *300 tournaments* in the course of his career! How many times have you failed in your life? Could you handle losing that many times? Would you be looking for a boat to leave the stormy island?

The Success Recipe

Outperform: *A funny thing happened during my massive failures...I became successful.*

The success recipe is simple - it only contains two ingredients:

1 – Fail repeatedly.
2 – Don't quit. Ever.

That's the difference between The Norm and Outperformers – willingness to fail and an explanatory style that bolsters confidence and resiliency.

If you're going to quit on the first sign of failure, don't even start. Keep crawling contently. Outperforming comes from being willing to fall as many times as it takes to learn to walk.

Why This vs. Why Me?

Guilt is one of the most useless emotions we experience. It binds us to the past. Whatever we feel guilty about is done and there's nothing we can do to change it. We need to move on.

I'm not saying that we shouldn't be remorseful if we've done something wrong, but I am saying that beating ourselves up over it is not going to help anything. It is only going to make us feel worse.

Feeling guilty almost always stems from a *Why Me* attitude.

We get really angry with someone. *Why did I do that? Why me?*

We get fired from a job. *What did I do wrong? Why me?*

We get hurt in a relationship. *How could this happen? Why me?*

We gain ten pounds. *Where is my willpower? Why me?*

Instead of using the woeful *Why Me* attitude, switch to a *Why This* attitude. Ask yourself, why is THIS happening. Focus on understanding the problem first by looking at your past thoughts and actions. When you do this, you'll start actively generating solutions instead of dwelling on the guilt from thinking about yourself.

You get really angry with someone. *Why This?*

- You've had a stressful day. The person annoys you. You got a bad night's sleep. Simple miscommunication. Something building up over time.

You get fired from a job. *Why This?*

- Company is downsizing. You're underperforming. You're better off elsewhere. Corporate politics. Boss has it in for you. Bad fit with your skill set.

You get hurt in a relationship. *Why This?*

- You weren't compatible. You misread some signals. They were getting back at you for something you did. Bad timing. The person is a dirt bag.

You gain ten pounds. *Why This?*

- You weren't consistent with your exercise program. Too many desserts. Stress. Poor planning. Bad time management. Lack of support system.

Note, every one of these is about understanding WHY something happened and generating possible solutions for the problem. A *Why Me* attitude would mope around, saying, "I'm a hothead. I'm not smart. I'm worthless. I'm a failure." That attitude gets you nowhere.

Conditioning Your Personal Power

If you fail enough times in your life, with the wrong explanatory style, you can acquire learned helplessness, which means you believe that NOTHING you do will ever change your outcome. Your motivation, your thinking and your emotions are all sapped. You are helpless.

Outperform: *You can condition helplessness or you can condition power. It's your CHOICE.*

Last year, I started working with a very high level runner. I didn't know it at the time, but her friends had basically forced her to contact me. I could tell she was skeptical in our initial meeting. She thought I was full of sh*t and there was nothing I could do to help her.

She was 46 years old and had only been running for a few years. When she first started running, she saw amazing results. Her times would get faster, literally, on every run. She couldn't have been happier with her progress. She thought it would never end.

Then she hit a plateau. NOTHING she did would make a difference. She would change her eating – same results. She would change her training – same results. She would change her race strategy – same results. Every time she set a goal for a race, she would fall short.

She developed learned helplessness and was on the verge of quitting running.

So, I convinced her to give me a 90-day commitment. I assessed where she was and I wrote up her training program. And I'll never forget one of the first things she said to me when she looked at it, *"really, that's all the farther you want me to run?"*

Of course she was skeptical – I had cut her training volume by 25%. Remember the *MED* from the Health section? I'm all about minimizing time and maximizing efficiency.

Most people would think if you want to run better you either need to train faster or train longer, but running is no different than anything else in life – it's a game of confidence (especially when it comes to racing). Your training doesn't matter if you're not confident you can execute when it matters most. Mind over matter. The mentally strong athlete ALWAYS wins.

The cure to learned helplessness is to develop *power*. The way to develop power is to build confidence. The way to develop confidence is through accomplishments...no matter how small. Stack enough accomplishments together and you'll have confidence and power to change any outcome.

In her case, by cutting her training volume and focusing on accomplishing small goals, one at a time, she got her confidence back. And just like you would condition the body to lift heavier weights over time, the size of her accomplishments increased as well.

She set personal bests in every race that season. And she's just getting warmed up. The best is yet to come.

Power Posture

I've talked enough athletics throughout the course of this book so I may as well stay with the theme. Think about what athletes do every time they're victorious in competition. What do they do? What is their posture?

Now think about someone in your life who is negative, depressed and, in general, a Debbie Downer. What do they look like? What is their posture?

Next question – were these postures taught to us in school? I don't know about you but I don't ever remember my teacher or coach telling me that I should speak louder, throw my arms up, stick my chest out and look to the sky when I do something good. I also don't remember anyone telling me that I should slump forward, look down and talk softly when I'm having a bad day.

We do these things *instinctively*. These postures coincide perfectly with specific emotions. And if you're wondering where I'm going with this, you guessed it – you can actually CREATE these emotions by mimicking the given postures. Changing the way you hold your body will, actually, change the physiological feelings inside of your body.

The top 4 ways to condition your personal power:

1 – Spend less time sitting. Stand up and walk around, as often as possible. Every time we sit, we're in a protracted, restricted posture. And it affects our emotions. At the bare minimum, stand up and walk around every hour (hopefully, you're hydrated enough where you'll *have to* do this). If you want personal power, walk briskly, with purpose. Like you're a man (or woman) on a mission who knows exactly what they are going to do and how it's going to get done. This will transfer into your actions.

2 – Stretch out your chest, hamstrings and hip flexors. Do this at least 3 times per day, preferably once in the morning, once in the afternoon and once in the evening, holding the stretches for at least 30 seconds at a time.

Doing this will not totally counteract the hours spent sitting down but it will keep it as manageable as possible. Yoga is always a great option for stretching as well...in addition to stress relief.

3 – Scream and yell like you just hit the game winning shot. Do *exactly* what you would do if you were a professional athlete and you just won the world championship. Throw your arms in the air, stick your chest out and let out a resounding, "YESSSSS!" Of course, you'll probably have to do this when no one is around or they may think you're crazy. But, even if people are around, the more of it you can mimic, the better. And before you dismiss it as whacko – just try it. It WILL affect how you feel, your confidence and your level of personal power. When is the last time that you screamed and yelled like you're the king (or queen) of the world?

4 – Create anchors. Anchoring can be a very powerful tool if used correctly. It is a more modern technique that is used to condition (or "anchor") a desired emotional state *instantly*, on command. Athletes, musicians and speakers frequently use anchoring in preparation for performances or during key moments to access an emotional state. You can do the same thing.

Here's what you do:

First, choose what emotion you want to anchor. It can be confidence, empowerment, positivity, alertness, excitement, or literally, anything else.

Second, choose how you're going to anchor the emotion. You can do many things but, personally, I like to press my thumb and forefinger together. You have to choose something that is unique and that would not *normally* happen during your daily routine.

Third, take a trip down memory lane when you had, and felt, the exact emotion you were looking for. Close your eyes (if possible) and try to remember the situation as vividly as possible (sights, sounds, smells, etc.). Get to a place where you feel the strong emotion, then double the intensity. And double it again. The stronger you feel the emotion, the better.

Fourth, when you have reached an extremely strong emotional state, press HARD on your anchor for 3-5 seconds. Release and do this again. Be sure to repeat the third and fourth steps each time and to make sure you're at a strong emotional state *before* pressing your anchor.

To make anchoring effective, you have to BRING IT. You can't go through the motions and "kinda" feel a state. It won't work. Don't press the anchor until you've consciously tried to double the intensity at least once.

It's funny; my first personal experience with anchoring came from driving to Chicago from Minnesota to go to a Maroon 5 concert (my girlfriend's idea – I was seeking brownie points). It's about a 7-hour drive and I was already tired, and I knew it wouldn't get any better once we got to the concert. I didn't figure yawning through the entire concert would score me any points so I decided to take my shot at anchoring. So, for almost the entire drive to Chicago, I anchored presence and alertness. I sat up in my seat, remembered some of the races I've done where I've felt most alive and focused, and worked hard to anchor that state in exactly the way I just mentioned.

And, amazingly, it worked. Every time I felt like I was getting tired at the concert, I just pressed my thumb and forefinger together, HARD. And each time I did that, I immediately got more focused and present. That was enough to personally sell me on anchoring...and I've since taught it and seen it work for plenty of others.

Doing any of these four things ensures that, in addition to conditioning your psychology with the proper mindset and thought patterns, you'll also be conditioning your physiology for success and personal power. Both are important in their own unique ways and, when used together, is an outperforming combination.

We all get beat down every now and then. We get fragile. We internalize. We feel guilty.

First, focus on your explanatory style. Become *aware* of how you explain positive and negative events in your life. You cannot change something you're not aware of.

Second, embrace mistakes. Every time you make a mistake, and learn something from it and realize it has brought you one step closer to success. Make enough mistakes and you'll find whatever level of success you desire. The highest levels of success require the greatest number of mistakes. That's the Price of Admission.

If life has beaten you up like a punching bag – focus on getting wins. It DOESN'T MATTER how small. Any wins constitute positive momentum moving forward. And when you get these wins, don't be dismissive about it. Stand up and recognize that you're the one who made it happen. No one else – just you. YOU were capable. YOU got the job done.

Remember – confidence is arrogance under control.

Outperform: *Life is a boxing match. Don't stand passively in the corner. Hit back!*

It drives my clients crazy when they thank me for their successes and I respond, *"I didn't do anything - YOU did all the work."*

I don't say this because I'm uncomfortable with accepting praise. It actually feels really good to be appreciated. I do it because I want people to have the confidence to know they can do it on their own, with no one watching and without me there. It's giving them the autonomy to know they control their outcomes. It's their choice. It's their life.

It's yours, too.

OUTPERFORM NOW:
High Performance

1. What's your island? How far away is it? What are the people like? The weather? The wealth? The health? This will get your mind going in the right direction...

2. What *specifically* in your life do you want to accomplish? What is the Price of Admission tied to it? Write down the discipline and dedication and sacrifices it would realistically take for you to get it done and ask yourself, *honestly*, if you're willing to pay it. If you're not, revise. If you are, get to work.

3. Write down everything you're afraid of and everything that is holding you back. Be introspective. Next, write down all of these fears with a, "What if [insert positive statement]" after it. Keep these statements somewhere that you can see them *daily*.

4. What area(s) of your life would you like to go from The Norm to Outperform? What are the fundamentals? Which fundamentals are you lacking? What are your strengths? What are your weaknesses?

5. Based on your current schedule, allocate "blocks" or "chunks" of time that you can use to develop your fundamentals. Try to make these chunks at least 90 minutes to 2 hours in length.

6. Identify 2 or 3 of the 12 *Focused Productivity* strategies and start using them immediately.

7. Determine your best mediums for inspiration. From a psychological conditioning standpoint, we ALL need this. Keep them on hand and use them anytime you need to get "game ready." Morning is a great time for this jumpstart.

8. Identify the events in your life that had the biggest effect on your self-confidence – what was your explanatory style? How could it have been improved and what will you tell yourself to handle it differently in the future?

9. What's your *Success Recipe*? What are you committed to failing at repeatedly and never quitting until it is DONE?

10. Choose ways you can start ingraining your "power posture." Use anchoring and begin practicing how to condition outperforming emotions on command.

HAPPINESS

Happiness is a fluid state, meaning that it changes from moment to moment. Unfortunately, no one stays happy all the time. We create it and lose it...more times than we imagine or care to realize. But when we're there, we know it. We feel it. Our lives change...if only momentarily.

Intuitively, this makes sense...

When we're happy, we have less sickness and better health.

When we're happy, we get in fewer arguments and our relationships improve.

When we're happy, we waste less time and get more done.

When we're happy, we earn more.

(yes, studies validate all of these findings)

Outperform: *Know what makes you happy and create it. Daily.*

So, all we have to do is get happy and every area of your life will improve, right? Not so fast.

Is it possible that better health might make you happier? Or improved relationships might make you happier? Same thing with productivity or financial abundance? You can easily get in a "chicken and the egg" debate over happiness but one thing is certain - defining happiness is difficult because it's subjective. There is no blanket solution that provides mass happiness. What makes me happy won't necessarily move the needle for you. It's individual, and like other talents and skills, some people find it "easier" to be happy than others. Many people don't even *know* what makes them happy.

These chapters are not geared towards what I would call "traditional happiness," which means I will not tell you to sit around and think happy thoughts because everything will always work out. That's false (or fake) happiness, like you're trying to convince yourself of something that you know isn't true. Every single person reading this book has probably gone through a period in their life where they were extremely unhappy...or downright sad...and all the positive thinking in the world wouldn't have changed their state. Things work out because you MAKE decisions and MAKE them work out, and with this, comes happiness. It's a proactive process.

Outperform: *To find happiness, actions speak louder than words...and thoughts.*

Now, I'm not discounting the need for positive thinking. When we get the flu and we're at home in bed, we can either bitch and moan about how bad we have it or we can honor the fact that we still have countless blessings in our lives and this too shall pass. We also have the open-ended opportunity to change our thoughts at any point in time. How we think about our current situation DOES matter. It's the backbone of positive psychology.

What I am discounting is *passivity* in positive thinking. Throwing our arms up in the air and waiting for life to make things better, with no positive ACTIONS on our part, doesn't work. It doesn't matter how many happy thoughts we think. We shouldn't leave our happiness up to fate. It should be left up to decided action.

The dictionary definition of happiness is *"The state of being happy."* Only one word matters in this definition: <u>state</u>. By now, you should know that states are something we can *create* at any moment. We need to capture it and seize it. Happiness is not something that we hope for – it's something that HAPPENS based on the way we live our lives and our daily activities.

These chapters are about the specific actions you can take to create greater levels of happiness in your day-to-day life. Outperforming is great, but what does it matter if you're not happy or having any fun doing it? That's empty success. We're after significance.

There are three fundamental components to outperforming happiness: our level of contribution, our desire for progress and growth, and our willingness to take risks.

CONTRIBUTION

One in Six Billion

You're one of a kind and completely unique. There are 6 billion people on the planet and, all the way down to your cellular DNA, there has never been someone built like you and there never will be again. Ever. No one else can do what you do, exactly the way you do it. This isn't a bullshit line of positive reinforcement – it's absolutely true.

At the risk of sounding preachy, I once heard someone say, "What you've been given (brains, skills, talents, etc.) is a gift *FROM* God; what you do with it is a gift *TO* God."

I wholeheartedly agree.

I don't reference this as my personal endorsement of a particular religion – it is more to symbolize that we're ALL given great gifts from the time we are born and it's up to us what we want to do with them. We can waste them through fear or greed or laziness or procrastination or excuses, or we can squeeze every last drop out of it and leave our stamp of contribution on the world. It's your call. Which would you rather have?

I majored in psychology in college and we used to debate nature versus nurture constantly. Which one is more important? How do the two interact? What are the defining characteristics of each that cause people to travel down certain paths...good or bad?

These are VERY difficult questions to answer.

Obviously, traits you are born with alludes to *nature*. What you DO with it is based on *nuture*. The reality is it is a complex interaction of both...but I do know one thing – only one of them is changeable.

Nature is fixed – you cannot choose your parents and your genes. And if you're reading this, you're probably a grown adult, so the nurturing process through adolescence is also fixed. But what I'm talking about is your ongoing "nurturing" through adulthood. It matters and it's determining much of your happiness right now.

I've worked with hundreds of clients over the past 12 years, and sometimes, we can all be guilty of wishing for things we don't have:

I wish I looked like this person.

I wish I were smart like that person.

I wish I had that job, car, or house.

Outperform: *Happiness is recognizing and contributing with the things you DO have.*

We've all been blessed with vast gifts and opportunities – we just need to realize it, never take it for granted, never stop working hard and always, *ALWAYS*, make the most of it. I have a belief that someday we'll be judged (to a certain extent) by how we used our gifts, to contribute to the greater good, in our time here on earth. We were put here to help others.

A few years ago, I was lucky enough to hear Lou Holtz (former Notre Dame football coach) lecture and he described how people nowadays are too concerned with their rights and privileges, whereas in previous generations people were more thoughtful of their responsibilities and obligations. In short, are we asking for things we did not EARN? Are we wanting things GIVEN to us without having to put in the work? And if we adopt this mindset where we see it as a responsibility and obligation to contribute by using our strengths, we'll be more content with who we are and where we're going.

Now, there's nothing wrong with striving for what we don't have and wanting to be something greater than we are today. Commitment, motivation and determination

<u>require</u> this mentality. We have to be uncomfortable (or disgusted) with where we are to progress. Otherwise we stand still, maintaining our position. The discomfort...or disgust...creates a sense of urgency for action.

However, there is a distinct difference between being intrinsically motivated by growth and development while still being appreciative of our gifts, and wanting to be something more while being angry with where we are, what we have and what we've been given. Even if we have nothing, we should still have an abundance mindset. Instead of saying, "I *wish* I...," say, "I'm *going to*..."

A fundamental truth of a contribution-based mindset is to never stop trying to be better for tomorrow, but don't forget to be appreciative and thankful for what you have today.

Life is a Team Sport

Growing up, golf was my first love. My mom used to drop me off at the golf course and I would play from dawn to dusk. I loved competing against myself to get better...and the fact that I was 100% responsible for every shot I hit. In this way, golf can teach you a lot about life and accepting personal accountability.

When I wasn't playing golf, I was watching it. One of my favorite events to watch was the Ryder Cup, which pits the top American players against the top European players. The announcers and players would always talk about the pressure and how it was unlike anything they'd experience in regular individual tournament golf. It was not until I started studying sport psychology in graduate school that I finally understood why...

They were playing for something greater than themselves.

When I say this, I'm actually not referring to the patriotic aspect of playing for your country (though this is certainly powerful) – I'm talking about playing for your TEAM. I guarantee if you asked a player why he was so nervous over a 4-foot putt to win the Ryder Cup, it wouldn't be because he was afraid of letting his entire country down. Even if they say that, it's a surface answer. The real reason players feel so much pressure is because they don't want to let their *team* down. All the players are standing there watching, relying on them, and believe it or not, it's a lot easier to accept letting yourself down than letting down a team comprised of your country's top players.

This intense pressure is caused by an overwhelming desire for contribution. There is nothing that makes you feel happier than when you've contributed to others. It has less to do with receiving praise that you did well – it's about knowing that you contributed. You were important. You mattered.

Outperform: *Happiness comes from contributing more to WE than ME.*

Life is a team sport. We're surrounded by "teams" everywhere. For many of us, family is the most important team. Maybe it's kids or maybe it's just your wife, but you'll try harder for them than you ever would for yourself. You'd lie down in traffic for your family. You need to provide for them and they rely on you...physically, emotionally, financially. You don't want to let them down.

Companies function the same way. The highest performing businesses are the ones that have developed a culture not of a hierarchy, but of a team. Even if the corporate structure has titles and bosses and direct reports – this is not the company feeling. In fact, you can usually recognize it because the titles will read "team member" (or something similar) instead of, "assistant manager" or "manager." Everyone is seen on a level playing field...from the executives, to the assembly line workers, to the customer service reps answering the phone. EVERYONE matters. EVERYONE must contribute for the team to be successful.

I used to work in sales as a regional account manager and we all tried harder if we felt the team needed our sales to hit our collective target than if we were only worrying about our individual quotas. I've never felt more pressure (and more subsequent happiness) if I delivered on the last day of the month because I knew our team was counting on me. It was like I drained the putt on the 18th hole to win the Ryder Cup. Numerous other studies in business show the same thing.

In fitness, this is part of the reason group classes can be so successful. If the right group comes together you can build a team-like atmosphere. This increases your motivation to attend because you don't want to let the "team" down. Whether it is reality or not, you feel they are relying on you. They're holding you accountable. Corporate weight loss challenges (where teams or departments compete against each other) work exactly the same way.

Think of those who have contributed the most to our society – Steve Jobs, Mother Theresa, Abraham Lincoln, Martin Luther King Jr., etc. – do you really think they would have accomplished what they did if they were only focused on what was best for them and not on contributing to society as a whole? Their desire for contribution drove them to be more than they ever would have been on their own.

Outperform: *Motivation comes from focusing on who **needs** your contribution.*

Recent studies in sport psychology have shown that the highest performing athletes almost always display the most gratitude, which means they are thankful for all they've been given (skills, genetics, hand-eye coordination, etc.) and they want to use their talents to contribute in the greatest way possible. They wake up *wanting* to work hard because they, literally, feel like they owe it to themselves, and others, to do so. Instead of coming from an attitude of lack, they are coming from an attitude of abundance.

Contrast this with other athletes who have comparable gifts that never succeed. We all know stories of the top draft pick who gets a lot of money thrown at them but never amounts to anything. Their talents are squandered. Why? What's changed?

It baffles me how far behind the major sports are with what truly motivates people. You want to know whether an athlete will excel? Stop poking and prodding and precisely measuring their speed, strength, agility, power, explosiveness and endurance. Athletes aren't rats in a lab. Start looking at how happy they are, how grateful they are for what they've been given and how much desire they have to contribute. Intangibles matter when it comes to happiness and high performance.

Outperform: *Money makes you more of what you were before you had it.*

Shortly before I ran the Twin Cities Marathon (my second marathon), my mother and a good friend of hers, Carol, were diagnosed with breast cancer. Considering 1 in 8 women will be diagnosed with breast cancer at some point in their lives, this may not seem alarming. But when you come from Albany, MN, population 1701, the chances of two friends, of almost the same age, getting breast cancer at the same time is highly unlikely. It rocked the town and it certainly rocked my emotions.

The only difference? My mother was diagnosed stage 2 and Carol was diagnosed stage 4. My mother went through chemo and radiation and is still alive today. Carol went through chemo and radiation but passed away within one year. God rest her soul.

I have no idea why things worked out like they did. The situations could have so easily been reversed. But I stopped contemplating the "what ifs" and started focusing on how I could potentially contribute and give back. So, I decided to raise money for an organization called *City of Hope* that does groundbreaking research for cancer and diabetes in conjunction of my running the marathon. People contributed over $4,000 and it was one of the happiest, most empowering experiences of my life. To this day, it's the second fastest marathon I've ever run.

Outperform: *You'll always try harder when it's for something greater than yourself.*

We can all be guilty of holding back from time to time and not giving 100%. Maybe we feel like we don't know enough or we're not ready. Maybe we're afraid what people will think of us. Maybe we just get off course and struggle to get back on. Maybe we've just gotten lazy and need a swift kick in the ass. Specific strategies for these things were discussed in the *High Performance* section but the fastest way to take massive positive action is to focus on nothing other than your contribution. It also pays to think of who you'll be letting down and what you'll LOSE if you don't contribute (a very powerful motivator).

If you're in business, who benefits from your products? Customers? Community? Society? Work to a point where you will do *anything* to get your product or service in their hands because you know how much it will benefit them. Also, think of all the people you'll be letting down if your business fails (not only your customers, but your employees, vendors and everyone you provide for).

If you're struggling to follow an exercise program, think of how much better a person you'll be if you're healthy...personally and professionally. Conversely, you can also think of how much you'll be letting people down if you don't take care of yourself. If you can't play with your kids when you get home from work because you're dogged tired, do something about it. You have people relying on you to be your best.

If you want to be happier on a day-to-day basis, focus on a continual contribution to others. This can be family, charity, business, community, friends or just society as a whole. But get out of your own way and break from your own bubble. Make others better. Make the world better. Do this and I promise you'll have more peace in your heart and more happiness in your life.

Forgive But Never Forget

You cannot be an Outperformer if you're holding onto past grudges.

I found Michael Jordan's Hall of Fame induction speech fascinating. For those of you who didn't see it, look it up on YouTube. If you know anything about Jordan, you know that the bulk of his competitive desire came from proving people wrong. He was famous for not talking to (or "freezing out") someone in the media if they were a doubter or hater. He would target certain opponents if they did the same thing. He internalized everything and used it as fuel for his motivational fire to succeed.

In his speech, he started from the time he was cut as a high school sophomore and worked through his entire career, calling out every person who ever doubted him and basically said, *"Ha ha, I told you so!"* He reveled in the fact that he got the last laugh. At the time he was highly criticized for it, but I loved it. It wasn't scripted; it was 100% real, pure and authentic, which is a lot better than someone telling us what they think we want to hear.

But just because it was real doesn't mean I necessarily *agree* with his motivational tactics. Jordan obviously is the greatest basketball player of all time but I wonder, if you asked him and if he answered *honestly*, whether he is truly happy, what he would say?

Outperform: *If you can't learn to forgive, you may be successful...but you'll never be happy.*

When you hold onto anger, resentment and bitterness, they are like poisons in the body. These negative emotions are part of the reason why people who are unhappy are often sick and stressed. The poison in their body is silently killing them on the inside.

The problem with not forgiving is that it keeps us focused on what has gone *wrong* in our lives instead of what is currently going *right*. Now, don't get me wrong, you can be extraordinarily successful by holding onto these emotions, as is evidenced in the Michael Jordan example. Actually, quite a few high achieving athletes and business leaders make it to the top by seeking retribution for everyone who has ever doubted or questioned them. It causes them to arrive earlier, stay later and bust their ass when no one is watching or seems to care.

But when they finally do reach whatever level of success they're seeking, at some point, they usually stop to smell the roses. And they don't smell nearly as sweet as they thought they would. They're missing something. It's not what they had imagined.

At this point, the high achiever can go one of two ways:

1 – they can be introspective and accept that there may be a better way to do things.

2 – they can continue plowing along, thinking that maybe they just haven't "made it" yet, but when they do, it will all be worth it and the roses will smell sweeter.

For the sake of their happiness, I hope they choose door #1.

Don't get me wrong; forgiveness is difficult. *Really difficult.* Like many things, it is a skill that must be learned and takes tremendous discipline to actively forgive people for wronging you. But I can promise you this – if you're willing to do it, you will feel a gigantic monkey be removed from your back. You will have a sense of freedom and peace that you've never felt before. You'll lose a huge amount of weight, figuratively speaking.

Now, I'm not saying you need to forget about it when something unfortunate happens to you. Lying down and acting like nothing has happened is not a good strategy either. There are countless stories of people being fired from companies and using it to come back stronger. Walt Disney was fired from the Kansas City Star in 1919 because he lacked imagination. Steve Jobs was fired from his own company, Apple, before coming back to grow it to unparalleled heights. Abraham Lincoln lost seven elections for public office before becoming president. But the big difference lies in how much you internalize the anger and resentment for what has happened to you and how much you use the lesson as something you can learn from with a positive desire to prove yourself. It's a fine line.

The single best way to forgive people is to take the high road. When someone wrongs you, it says a helluva lot more about them than it does about you. You're better than that. Strangely enough, when people are unappreciative, say or do nasty things or don't treat you with decency and respect, it's for ONE reason only:

They're unhappy with themselves.

Outperform: *Always stay on the happiness high road. The view is better up there.*

That's the bottom line. Let the unhappy people continue down their unhappy low road. Help them...or pray for them. Or let them go. Whatever you choose to do, forgive them and don't dwell on it – you've got outperforming to do.

The Big Five

There are a few other basic "fundamentals" that, when executed, will greatly enhance your happiness:

1. Choose Experiences Over Materials

Ask yourself something – when you think of the times in your life when you felt the happiest and the most alive, were you buying a material possession or experiencing a once-in-a-lifetime trip, adventure, concert or sporting event?

I can guess your answer.

Many recent studies show that experiences make people happier than materials. The reason is that, regardless of the cost or quality of the material possession, we will grow accustomed to it over time. It loses its novelty when we see it day after day after day. This acclimation process usually happens in the first two months of acquiring something new.

Experiences, on the other hand, fill us up. They are rare and you know it's not something you'll have every day so you hold onto it long after the event occurred. You cherish and appreciate it more. Photos and videos only enhance the memories...and you probably wouldn't trade them for anything in the world.

If you seek happiness, always choose to invest in experiences over materials.

2. Use Your Inherent Strengths

Do what you were put here to do. Maybe you've heard that before?

Talent is mostly overrated. You can make up for it with work ethic and skill development, and it doesn't matter if we're talking about business or athletics (or anything else). But we ALL have specific gifts with which we were born. If you're questioning what yours may be, they are the things that come easy to you but are hard for others. What someone else can do, you can do faster, easier and better. Everyone has these in spades.

Outperform: *Your greatest strengths are what come easy to you but are hard for others.*

Maybe you're a whiz with numbers or you're a born communicator who can sell anything, but you *know* what your strengths are – you don't need me to tell you. But I can tell you this – if you are *not* doing something that emphasizes your inherent strengths every single day, you will struggle to be truly happy...or achieve your greatest individual success. You'll lack the "mental paycheck" that comes from making a lasting contribution with the unique, specific gifts that God gave you and very few others on this planet. You'll be playing small.

If you've gotten trapped into doing something that doesn't utilize your strengths because it's what society told you you're "supposed to be doing," it's time to break out of it. The Norm is littered with regrets and wasted potential. Remember that person who went along with the crowd and was just like everyone else? I don't either.

The world needs you to step up your game. Outperforming comes from having the courage, and confidence, to be different and take the road less traveled. And when you're in a situation where you're able to use your inherent strengths to the fullest, you'll achieve greater levels of success because you're maximizing your productivity by doing what you do *best*. There's tremendous *value* in this, no matter the industry or profession.

3. Lose Yourself

Have you ever gotten so wrapped up in a project that you totally lost track of time? Or forgot to eat? Or neglected your pets? Or didn't even realize the coffee maker was burning?

I'm notorious for not noticing anything going on around me when I'm running. I remember one specific run a few years back when my brother and I were getting ready for yet another marathon. We had a 19-miler on the training schedule and we decided to loop through downtown Minneapolis to check on the progress of building Target Field (the Minnesota Twins stadium). The downtown loop came later in the run when I was locked into my "zone," and when we started coming out of downtown, I turned to my brother and asked, "where was the Twins stadium, anyway?" He looked at me with utter disbelief...like I had three heads. It was a massive gaping dirt hole and we had run around the entire perimeter. I didn't even notice it was there...I was just focused on the task at hand.

Outperform: *Losing yourself means you're fully immersed in what you're presently doing.*

Losing yourself in your daily activities is a key determinant of overall happiness. It happens when you become so engrossed in what you're doing that you don't even realize what's going on in the world around you. Sport psychology calls this phenomenon the "flow" state and it is very characteristic of what the highest performing athletes feel when they're able to tune out the crowd, the game slows down and everything feels easy. The periphery goes gray and the only thing in focus is what needs to get done. And it almost always translates to a peak performance.

Of course, this becomes difficult if you hate what you do and you don't *want* to lose yourself in what you're doing. If this is you, I can offer one helpful suggestion – focus more on your individual achievements and what you're accomplishing throughout the course of your day. If you struggle to focus at work, it's probably because you're no longer being challenged. Everything feels boring...and dull...and monotonous. Leave a piece of bread on the counter for a week and you'll see what I mean. You're stale.

If this sounds like you, find a way to challenge yourself. Make it a game. If you do the same thing every day, can you challenge yourself to get it done faster than you have before (smooth talk your boss to give you a reward for doing so!)? Or, can you come up with a different way of doing the same task that may be more beneficial? Or could you stretch yourself with an additional task that would make things more interesting? I know you're probably saying that you have enough to do as it is, but when you truly lose yourself in a task, your productivity increases because you're focused and you get more done in less time. It's a beautiful thing.

Much of being able to lose yourself in a task also comes from using your inherent strengths...and finding a task you find intrinsically enjoyable.

4. Get Fresh Air

Studies have actually shown that fresh air makes people happier. Just the act of being outside cleanses our lungs by oxygenating our blood. It also cleanses our mind by calming our thoughts. There's no better feeling than being outside when you've been stuck inside all day.

Outperform: *Fresh air is fuel for happiness and peak productivity.*

I sometimes refer to fresh air as the "magic cure all." I don't believe that we were made to be stuck in boardrooms and businesses all day. And I get that it's impossible to move all your meetings outside and to put a retractable roof on your office building. But as little as 15-20 minutes of fresh air can have a positive impact on your happiness. You'd be surprised how a walk outside in the morning, during a break at work, or around your neighborhood to close the day can have dramatic benefits.

5. Smile and Laugh More

This is probably the simplest of all – if you want to be happier, just smile and laugh more. Now, you may be asking, "what if there is nothing to smile or laugh at?" Actually, it doesn't matter. You can "fake it till you make it," to a certain extent, when it comes to happiness.

The muscles in the face that are used to smile and laugh trigger specific physiological responses that promote feelings of happiness. Crazy, but true. You can actually try it – the next time you're feeling really unhappy, just find an excuse to smile and laugh at anything you possibly can (I wouldn't recommend breaking this out at a funeral, though, or when your boss spills coffee on himself). Doing this repeatedly *will* improve your mood.

As an FYI – this can work the opposite way as well. If you frown and look sad, you will be less happy...regardless of what's going on in your life. So, choose your facial expressions wisely!

PROGRESS

Becoming the Best in the World

This quote by Jim Rohn is too good not to share:

"You must constantly ask yourself these questions: Who am I around? What are they doing to me? What have they got me reading? What have they got me saying? Where do they have me going? What do they have me thinking? And most important, what do they have me becoming? Then ask yourself the big question: Is that okay?"

I've been to a lot of presentations on personal development and self-improvement, and most people agree that you'll be the average of the five people closest to you. Stop and think about that for a second – who are you closest to? What effect (positive or negative) are they having on your life? Are they pulling you up or pushing you down?

Yes, you hear stories about people coming from nothing, making it big and overcoming all odds. But, in reality, these stories are few and far between. They are the exception and not the rule. The success *most* people have is directly proportional to the people with whom they choose to surround themselves.

This has been a personal goal of mine in the past few years. I used to be intimidated by people who were more educated than me, had more money than me, or were better spoken and more successful than me. I'd shrink in their presence. No more! I finally made the decision to spend as much time with positive and successful people as possible. I'm doing this because I believe it is human nature to want to fit into your environment…to not upset the pack. But by surrounding myself with people who pull me up I know I am making myself better.

Outperform: *Surround yourself with the people who are the best in the world at what you want.*

I'd strongly encourage you to do the same. If someone has something you want, spend as much time with them as possible. In a way, this is success by osmosis. It may be uncomfortable but it'll make you better (and happier) in the long run. You can't help but be better when you're surrounded by greatness. They make you step up your game. You can learn from them and let it fuel your motivation. Then take action. Always take action. If you do this you will achieve more and accomplish more than you've ever thought possible.

Embracing the Process

Process is defined as a series of actions or steps taken in order to achieve a particular end. A big component to being happy comes from an appreciation and an *embrace* of this process.

> **Outperform**: *It's about the journey, not the destination.*

A while back I heard Jason Witten (tight end for the Dallas Cowboys) talking about what it takes to be elite. He cited one of the key fundamentals as a willingness to embrace the process that goes into any desired outcome.

For football players with a desired outcome of getting to the NFL, some of this is built on the field but most of it is built in the weight room. Everything that professional athletes do, day in and day out, to be bigger, faster and stronger takes tremendous discipline and a willingness to accept the slow process of improvement. When you get to the elite level, as little as 1% can be the difference between being the best player in the league and being cut from your team and out of the game forever. Everything you do, matters. It's a long, painstaking process.

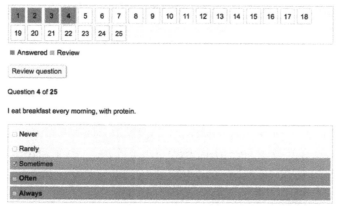

*Want to know how you're stacking up? Take this performance analysis at the **Outperformer's Vault**.*

OutperformTheNorm.com/Vault

The single biggest factor to embracing the process is to just get started. DON'T WAIT. Telltale signs that you're not embracing the process (and probably not happy either) sound like the following:

I will launch this business WHEN...

I will ask for this promotion WHEN...

I will begin exercising WHEN...

I will start eating better WHEN...

I will fix this relationship WHEN...

I will make time for this WHEN...

I will demand more of myself WHEN...

To go back to Jason's story, how absurd would it sound if he said, "I will start lifting weights WHEN I'm a professional football player." It's crazy. Lifting weights day after day, week after week, month after month, year after year, is what ALLOWS you to get into the NFL. It doesn't work the other way around (no cart before the horse here). But you have to start *somewhere*...and none of the business, health, relationship or time management strategies are any different.

Back when I was personal training, I used to hear this response semi-regularly when I'd meet with a new potential client:

"I'm going to get into shape first and then I'll come back and work with you."

Huh? What?

Here was my typical rebuttal:

"Do you go to a doctor when you're sick and say, 'Ya know, Doc, I'm going to go on my own and get healthy first, and then I'll come back to see you when I'm feeling better.'"

C'mon now - that doesn't make any sense. You work with a trainer to *get in shape*. You go to a doctor to *feel better*. You start the journey to *move closer* to your destination.

Part of having a successful *anything* is stepping in, stepping up and getting started. You need to know it may be a long, brutal process to get to your eventual destination. Part of progress, and ultimately, happiness, is taking one step forward towards your destination every single day. But *everybody*, in *every area*, had to start with the same first step.

Your Personal Standard of Excellence

Your personal standard of excellence is the expectations you have of yourself every single day of your life. This is your mantra, or mission statement, if you will. It's not influenced by society, your boss, your peers or anyone else. It is comprised of the way *you* choose to live your life.

Creating your own personal standard of excellence is simple. Just answer the following three questions, **daily**:

1. What 3 words will define my thoughts and actions today?

2. What will I never compromise?

3. What is one thing I'm committed to improving today?

These three questions have the power to shape your daily actions and your level of success and happiness in all areas of life. Make your answers BOLD. Great accomplishments come from great expectations...of yourself. Listen to your heart and forget about what you're "supposed to say." You're not serving the world by holding back.

Outperform: *Make everyone else come up to your level. Don't shrink to theirs.*

Elite athletes have lofty expectations placed upon them by teammates, fans and coaches. Business leaders have lofty expectations placed upon them by employees, peers and shareholders. Parents have lofty expectations placed upon them by their kids and spouse. And you don't have to be an elite level athlete, business leader or parent to know that these expectations can be stressful and crippling if your constant existence lies in trying to live up to other peoples' standards instead of your own.

Apple is a great example. Their mantra, as a company, is to innovate and think differently. They strive to be cutting edge and be better than anything else in the marketplace. These lofty standards have defined their explosive growth.

If someone at Apple were to answer the three questions, they might say something like this:

1. Innovative. Different. Excellence.

2. Quality.

3. Design and ease of use.

I always find Apple fascinating because their products are not only the most innovative, they're also the easiest to use (if my mom can use an iPad, *anybody* can do it). And they're beautifully designed. These are the reasons they are where they are.

But the BIGGEST reason for their success has been their willingness to go against the status quo. Think about it – since we were younger, we have been mostly suppressed to fit into a group structure, mostly starting in school. Educational institutions don't mean to do it, but the socialization and curriculums put more of an emphasis on the mistakes and setbacks (*"Why didn't I study more?"* or *"What went wrong out there?") and* how we stack up to others, rather than our own individual standards, desires and dreams. We, then, start to live our lives at a very early age consumed by social comparison and doing our best to fit into the group. We seek to perform at The Norm.

Outperform: *If you're reading this book, you're already in the top 1-2%.*

The best schools emphasize strengths first and focus on the individual, rather than the group as a whole (yes, I understand this can be difficult with the numbers). And the take home message from these schools is that we should put more weight on our own unique skills, talents and gifts, rather than thinking like all the rest. The fact is, if you're reading this book, you're already in the top 1-2% of all successful people. The great majority of people don't invest in personal development (they'd rather read trashy romance novels and celebrity gossip magazines) and of those that try, not all of them finish what they start. I commend you for making it this far. You're already thinking, and *acting*, differently.

True happiness comes from adhering to, and living your life congruently, with your personal standard of excellence, and feeling like you're doing everything in your power to be your unique, individual best each and every day.

RISKS

Take Your Shot

Every year I've made it a point to do
something really cool for my birthday. One
year I decided to hike the Grand Canyon. It
was something I always wanted to do and it
was time to cross it off my bucket list.

My birthday always falls right around Easter.
And, on that particular year, it happened to be
ON Easter. So, on a day that would normally
be reserved for time with family, that Easter
Sunday I set the alarm for 4:30am and drove
4.5 hours from the Las Vegas Strip to the South
Rim of the Grand Canyon. And as the
elevation went up and up and up, so too did
the anticipation. It was a great drive...watching
the sun come up over the desert. There wasn't
a cloud in the sky and I was stoked with
excitement.

When I got there, I realized the Grand Canyon
is really, *REALLY* big. Yes, this probably
sounds like the most blatantly obvious
statement you've ever heard but you cannot
possibly conceptualize just how big it is until
you're actually there. People on the trails

below you look like ants and the canyon looks like it stretches forever.

Now, the Grand Canyon is hard to hike but I was struck by how, in everything I read and all that I was given upon check-in, they were almost trying to beat it into you how difficult it was to hike. I finally understood why – in almost every other hike (to the top of a mountain, etc.) the hard part is going up initially at the start and the easier part is coming back on the way down. The Grand Canyon is the exact opposite. Most people hike far too deep into the canyon without having the foresight to think about how it's going to feel coming back up. And because there's barely any water…or shade…you're in for a long day if you don't prepare for it. And, trust me, it gets HOT as you start getting farther down the canyon.

Total, I hiked about 8 miles along the *Bright Angel Trail*. It did not disappoint. The biggest thing that struck me was how happy and friendly people were. I saw hundreds of people out that day and I could count on one hand the number of people who DID NOT say *"Good Morning," "Happy Easter,"* or *"Hello – How Are You?"* Unbelievable. How many people do this when you're walking around the grocery store, Target or the mall? I ended up ditching my iPod and soaking up the positive juju.

I had to drive another couple hours after I finished so I had a lot of time to think. I've often felt a "connection" with people who do this sort of thing. Words don't even need to be spoken – you can see it in their eyes. For the most part, the people going down the canyon were carefully watching their steps to make sure they didn't fall and the people going up were sucking wind and trying not to look up to see how much farther they had to go. But the look on their faces all said the same thing: *"There's no freekin' place on earth I'd rather be than in the Grand Canyon right now."*

This further solidified to me that I place far less value on THINGS than I once did - what I value the most are <u>moments</u> and <u>experiences</u>. And this isn't my push to turn you all into hikers and mountain climbers, but it is my push to make you think about <u>what truly makes you happy</u>.

I easily could have talked myself out of it and cancelled the trip. My girlfriend at the time was supposed to go with me but had an emergency at home and couldn't make it. It's probably not wise to embark on something like that by yourself. I actually think there are signs telling you not to go into the Canyon by yourself, but sometimes you've got to take action and take your shot. And, when it's over, you're always glad you did.

Outperform: *You miss 100% of the shots you don't take.*

Question for you...

What would make you get up in the middle of the night and drive for hours, just because it sounds like fun and you find it intrinsically enjoyable? Doing, trying or creating something? Traveling, experiencing or being somewhere? What would it take to get you out of the tunnel-vision crazy rat race of everyday life to look up and smile and say hello to every single person who walks by you? What needs to happen for you to have the look on your face that says *"There's no freekin' place I'd rather be than where I am right now?"*

The answers to these questions are keys to your overall happiness.

Developing Risk Tolerance

Much of the risks we take (or don't take) centers around our individual *Risk Tolerance*. It's impossible to assess where you currently are because your individual makeup and your perception and interpretation of the events in your life have heavily influenced your current willingness to take risks...in all areas of your life.

Now, please know when I'm speaking of risks, I'm talking about calculated risks that will stretch us, make us better and make us happier (going to Las Vegas and betting your life savings on Roulette doesn't qualify). The risks that matter are the ones that will genuinely improve your life and make you feel alive.

Your risk tolerance can be increased in one simple way – a greater focus on the benefits of doing accomplishing something versus the risk of attempting it. That's ALL you have to rationalize in your own head if you want to take more risks. If one outweighs the other, that's the decision you'll make.

So, in terms of the extreme Las Vegas example, there is a tremendous benefit to putting your life savings on red at the Roulette table and *winning*...BUT there is an even more substantial risk if you lose it. Most people have the common sense not to take that risk.

Still, most of the time, people are risk averse because they've had a bad experience with something in the past and it has left them scarred and filled with baggage. It closes their mind to new opportunities. It could be someone who has failed on a diet and is skeptical to give it another shot, it could be someone who has failed in business and is gun shy on trying it again or it could be someone who has been heart broken and mistreated in a relationship and is unwilling to put themselves back out there.

Outperform: *Risk tolerance is created by a constant focus on the benefits.*

The benefits of being successful on a diet include adding years to your life and life to your years. You'll have more energy for your family when you get home from work. You'll be more productive *at* work. You'll feel better about yourself. You'll no longer need to take medication. You'll be an example for people around you.

The benefits of starting your own business include financial freedom and impact. You'll have significance in the community. You'll have the ability to give back. You'll have something to pass along to your children. You'll be able to create jobs. You'll be happier doing what you *want* to do.

The benefits of finding a new relationship include intimacy and connection. You'll have someone with whom to share special moments. You'll have someone to confide in and grow closer to. You'll have someone to pick you up when you're feeling down.

When the benefits of your risk outweigh the potential consequences, you'll improve your risk tolerance. It's a teeter-totter and whichever side has more weight, wins. Like many things already discussed in this book, it's all about the way you choose to see it.

If you've taken a few large shots in the boxing match with life and you're an extremely conservative person, that's ok. Building risk tolerance can be built the same way you build a better body – through progressive overload. Just focus on gradually increasing your willingness to take risks by emphasizing the benefits and you will see the needle move over time. You'll be happier and you'll feel more alive. You'll wake up looking forward to whatever challenges life throws at you and you won't be afraid to confront them.

There are a couple simple rules to follow to develop risk tolerance...and here they are:

1. Say What You Mean. Mean What You Say.

Many of us live in a "woulda, shoulda, coulda" world. "I wish I would've said that," or "I should've said this," or "I could've done it differently." The same could also be said about "what ifs."

It is a regretful way to live.

Outperform: *Courage weighs ounces. Regret weighs tons.*

Many times we hold back what we really want to say because we fear conflict and want to avoid it at all costs. We don't want to rock the boat so we think it's better to suppress what we're really thinking and feeling, in favor of not offending anyone.

My brother and I often joke about being "Minnesota polite." Say that you're at a holiday with family – well, in Minnesota, you cannot just get up and leave. No no no no no! God forbid you're clear with your intentions! You have to pre-announce that you'll be leaving soon, make small talk, then announce that you'll be leaving shortly, make more small talk, stand up and slowly put on your shoes and jacket so everyone knows you're getting ready to leave while making even more small talk, THEN you're officially able to leave. *That* is Minnesota polite. Nobody gets offended. Ever.

A funny story but it's not far off from the truth.

When we hold things inside that we are honestly thinking or feeling, it builds bitterness and resentment. And when these things are held inside and swept under the rug, it's like poison trapped inside the body. It's toxic to our emotional, mental and physical wellbeing. Studies have shown that holding in these emotions can even have negative health consequences.

Outperform: *We are not meant to live life bottled up. Let it out already!*

When you make a commitment to honesty, you're also committing to occasional conflict...which is why most people don't do it. Many people fear conflict. But conflict brings resolution. It can also bring compromise and a deeper understanding and respect. But this will never happen if we're sitting around thinking one thing but doing another...all because we feel we need to be polite.

Say what you mean and mean what you say. It's freeing. After you've done this, won't it feel SO much better afterwards?

2. Be Courageous and Live Truthfully

Many people fear putting themselves out there. They fear rejection and don't want to be honest about who they really are. They'd rather be part of the crowd and fit into some societal norm than be ostracized for being, or trying, something different.

I remember going on a long run (about 12 miles) last summer. Super hot, super humid. The heat index was over 100 and there wasn't a cloud in the sky.

First, I don't know what I was thinking going on the run in the first place...but it was on my training calendar so I had to get it done (it was written in *ink*, after all). And when I finished the run I was tired, thirsty and dehydrated. And I was out in the suburbs so there wasn't any drinking fountains or water nearby.

Then, in an act of divine intervention, I noticed three kids setting up a lemonade stand about 50 yards down the road. At first I thought I was hallucinating but then I realized it was real. I was SAVED! I promptly stumbled over to them, gave them a $5 bill and drank their entire pitcher of lemonade. I guarantee they still made a solid profit.

Later, I started thinking about lemonade stands, conditioned responses and the way most of us resist putting ourselves out there and embracing new opportunities. We're too afraid of what may happen.

Now, I never actually asked the kids these questions (I was more concerned with drinking their lemonade) but I seriously doubt they thought any of the following in setting up their lemonade stand that day:

What will our friends say about us if we set up a lemonade stand?

What if our lemonade isn't as good as the other lemonade?

I don't think selling lemonade is my skill set.

Is now really the right time to be setting up a lemonade stand?

What will we do if no one shows up to buy our lemonade?

I don't want to come across as a pushy salesperson at my lemonade stand.

I'm really busy right now so I think I'm going to wait until SOMEDAY to set up my lemonade stand.

So, what has changed? What's different? If you've contemplated any of these questions in a new business venture, why are you no longer thinking like you did when you were a kid?

(I can hear you saying that you have more to lose now. No – you don't. Stop focusing on the negative. You actually have a helluva lot more to GAIN.)

Here's the deal - I'm guessing all the kids' thought about was:

1. It's really hot outside, and
2. People will want lemonade.

It's THAT simple. They had something that people wanted and they took action to do it. They didn't have to weigh the pros and cons – the biggest con was that nobody bought the lemonade and they drank it themselves. Big deal. At least they had the courage to take the shot.

Outperform: *What's your "lemonade stand" and what's stopping you from setting it up?*

Please understand, it's really hot outside (figuratively speaking) and you probably have something great that people want...and that people *need*. And you are compromising yourself by not offering it to others. It shouldn't matter if there isn't another lemonade stand set up within 100 miles...what matters is that you have the courage to get out there and take your shot. And I'm not just talking about business – I'm talking about generously giving more of YOURSELF.

Choosing Happiness

At any moment in your life, you can choose to be happy. Yes, *choose*. Happiness is a decision. A perception. A conscious thought. It is not a right or a privilege or something that just magically pops up out of thin air. You make yourself happy because you choose to be that way.

Outperform: *Happiness happens because you make it happen.*

Think about the amount of <u>your</u> individual happiness that rests upon the actions of others. All of it? Most of it? Some of it?

Any amount of it is too much.

How many times have you said, *"God, that person just makes me soooo mad!?"*

Question: *Who controls whether you get mad?*

Answer: *You do.*

You control every single emotion in your life, including happiness. No one can make you feel a certain way unless you choose to let them. You also control all of your choices and decisions based on these emotions.

Once you come to grips with the fact that happiness is 100% in your control, it's freeing and empowering. Happiness is something you find – happiness isn't something that finds you.

Outperform: *Happiness is proactive, not reactive.*

Now, I get it – certain spontaneous emotions and reactions are going to happen based on what others do to us. It's human nature. Deep down, all of us want to be loved, accepted, recognized, appreciated, etc. We're not mindless robots.

But when these reactions become problematic is when we dwell on them and let them fester, unable to let them go. The truly happy, healthy, high performing people don't differ dramatically in their initial emotional reactions – they differ in how they RESPOND to them. In other words, they recognize negative emotions are paralyzing, put them in their unconstructive place and move on.

You probably notice by now that I'm talking about living a life of anti-victimization. You're only the victim of something if you CHOOSE to be. Otherwise, it's just an unfortunate circumstance that you've put behind you and moved on from. It never sets you back. You've got outperforming to do.

Have you ever had something happen to you that you just couldn't move past? Usually, this is a breakup, job loss, injury or death or some other tragedy. I've had it happen to me many times...in all those areas. I can tell you every job I've ever gotten fired from and every girl that has ever dumped me. And before I realized the paralyzing thought processes I was putting myself in, it used to hold me back from moving on exploring new opportunities.

I still remember getting fired from a bartending job when I was in graduate school. Really, *bartending*? I did it all through undergrad as well...but when you're in graduate school you kind of feel like you should be past that point. But, so it goes, and I had to bills to pay. Meager graduate assistantship wasn't enough to live off.

I only had the job for about 3 weeks and I got fired. Actually, I wasn't fired – I was politely told I was "no longer needed." Uh huh. Is that supposed to make me feel better?

In retrospect, I never really "fit in." I was the ONLY one working there who wasn't from that area and didn't have the deep southern drawl. And I didn't even like the people...or the food...or the bar, for that matter. But that still didn't make it any easier. There were hundreds of other places in the area I could have gotten a new gig at but I couldn't move on. I was seriously bitter and I stewed over it for a few weeks.

I've had dozens of unfortunate things (personally and professionally) happen to me since then but "no longer being needed" still rings clearly in my mind. I'm guessing you may have a similar story. At some point, something probably happened to you that made it very difficult to move on. But, at some point, you CHOSE to do it, and once you did, everything changed...for the better.

Share Your Experiences

I'll never forget doing my second Ironman. The first one went by in a blur of pain and survival. All I cared about was crossing the finish line with a smile and a pulse.

The second one was about time. I wanted to do less than 11 hours and I trained HARD. I was living in Colorado at the time (yes, training at altitude helps) and I dedicated my entire summer to getting ready for that one day in September.

Fast forward to the finish line where I executed almost a perfect race, chopped 90+ minutes off my time from the year before and crossed the finish line in 10:51:49. I had a bunch of friends there supporting me and we all went out and had a great time afterwards.

On the flight home the next day I reflected on the race. On one hand, I felt a deep sense of satisfaction for my accomplishment but I realized that what made it truly special was having supportive friends to share it with afterwards. I drafted an emotional email to all of them on the plane because I wanted them to know how much I appreciated it. It wouldn't have meant nearly as much without them there.

Outperform: *Accomplishments mean less when you're alone.*

Ironman is a huge time commitment. Swimming, biking and running 15-20 hours a week can mean A LOT of time away from your friends (unless your friends are out there with you!). Business can consume us in exactly the same way. We get caught up in what we're doing and before you know it, months and *years* can go by where you haven't seen some of the friends you consider CLOSE. It's crazy how time flies.

Happiness comes from spending time with friends. Businesses will pass and so will accomplishments. Most of us don't remember moments – we remember moments and whom we were WITH. The moments you'll remember most are the ones you spent with your friends.

Pursue Your Hopes and Dreams

I started my own business when I was 32 years old. At the time, I had a great job with a global leader in training computers and fitness assessment technology. I was a Regional

Account Manager, was making very good money (I wasn't going to be buying an island anytime soon, but I was more than comfortable), loved our products and the people with whom I worked.

Why would I ever leave this situation?

Simple – I had greater hopes and dreams.

Trust me, I didn't just wake up one day and decide to put in my two-weeks notice. I contemplated it for at least a year before I finally had the courage to do it. And throughout this contemplation process, I rationalized every possible reason why I should NOT leave to start my own business. I was throwing away my steady paycheck, growth in my 401k, benefits, security, "perks" (like access to new products coming to the market, which I LOVED) and the opportunity for career advancement.

This is the way most of us evaluate new opportunities. We try to be as objective as possible, but what we REALLY do is see our new opportunities as great unknowns and drum up all supporting evidence to keep us where we are. We are creatures of habit. Even if we're not happy with our current circumstances, it's still often not enough to make us change. We'd rather stay unhappy where we are than to change and risk the unknown...even if the unknown may be better.

Truthfully, my hopes and dreams started as far back as graduate school, where I wrote a paper for a Sport Management class on a concept called Mind-Body Fusion, which would integrate the psychology and physiology necessary to help people achieve peak performance and live their best life. I was 24 when I wrote about this, so technically, you could say I had stalled on pursuing my hopes and dreams for 8 years.

Either way, after rationalizing why I should not start my own business for longer than I care to acknowledge, I started to flip the switch and look at things from a different perspective. I started to look at why I SHOULD start my business and why now was absolutely the right time (I was young, passionate, experienced, had no dependents, etc.).

Interestingly, I remembered a former boss of mine telling me the story of a paradigm shift. The story goes, a man and his two children get on the subway in New York City. The children are screaming and crying and are basically out of control. The father sits slumped down in his seat, without saying or doing anything. Finally, this goes on long enough where one of the passengers gets fed up and snaps at the father, *"why don't you control your kids so the rest of us can have some peace and quiet!?"* The father turns to the passenger and says sadly, *"I'm very sorry, sir. We just came from their mother's funeral. She passed away unexpectedly and we have no idea what to do."*

How do you think the passenger felt at that moment? Probably like a jack ass...and all it took was a simple paradigm shift to make him realize this.

Outperform: *A closed-minded camera lens results in missed opportunities.*

We are all conditioned to see the world from a certain perspective. Think of it as a lens on a camera. You have one that is probably the most comfortable for you...but that doesn't mean it's necessarily the best one to use for a given picture. Sometimes the settings need to be adjusted to see things differently and to open your eyes to the possibilities.

Most people never pursue their hopes and dreams because they are unwilling, or unable, to see the situation from a different perspective. I see it every day. And it's sad because it also means a very small percentage of the population actually achieves their fullest potential and lives a life of true happiness. We get complacent in performing to the expectations of others and keep putting things off until it's too late.

As you're reading this, is there something in your life you've been putting off that you've ALWAYS wanted to do? It can be something on your bucket list, whether it's personally or professionally. What has stopped you from doing it? You don't have enough time? You're worried about money? You lack confidence and belief in yourself?

None of these things are valid reasons unless you have a concrete plan to improve them. If you don't have enough time now, please outline for me your plan to *create* more time in the future (good luck with that one). If you're worried about money, what's your plan to *create* enough wealth that you won't have to worry about money, so you can then embark on your hopes and dreams? If you lack confidence in yourself, how are you personally investing in yourself to *create* different psychological beliefs?

Don't let these excuses hold you back from pursuing your hopes and dreams. Outperformers see opportunities and rewards whereas The Norm sees obstacles and risks. As always, you choose the camera lens.

OUTPERFORM NOW: Happiness

1. Write down your unique gifts. What makes you 1 in 6 billion? Don't sell yourself short – what are you grateful for and what are your inherent strengths and talents? Think from an attitude of abundance.

2. Whose "team" are you playing for? Who (or what) do you contribute to? Who needs you? Who relies on you?

3. Who do you need to forgive in your life? What grudges do you still hold onto? Remember, I'm not telling you to *forget* about these things but once you can come to grips with it, take the high road and move on, a gigantic weight will be lifted from your shoulders.

4. What do you want to *experience*? What's on your bucket list? What would you like to see? Do? Be a part of? When will you make it happen?

5. What would it take for you to "lose yourself" in your daily life? What would need to happen personally? Professionally? How can you get more present and lost in the process?

6. Identify the people you choose to surround yourself with – are they helping you get to where you want to go? Are they The Norm or Outperformers? Do they pull you up or down? Make you a better person or worse? What effect do they have on you? If you seek more in your life, surround yourself with people who have what you want.

7. Take a minute and think about the process and the journey you're going through – are you soaking it up? Are you appreciative of the little things? Are you embracing the process on the way to mastery...or complaining because it's hard or taking too long?

8. What's your *Personal Standard of Excellence*? Write it down and keep it somewhere where you can see it DAILY. Good places are your wallet/purse, bathroom, bedside, or your car.

9. What do you want to take your shot at but you haven't yet? Are you living courageously? Are you living your truth? Or are you conforming to society? To be happy, don't be afraid to take the road less traveled.

10. How can you *Choose Happiness*? Are you CHOOSING it? Or are you just hoping for it? What daily actions can you take to be happier? Who can you share the experiences with? What brings you true happiness?

CONCLUSION

I cnduo't bvleiee taht I culod aulaclty uesdtannrd waht I was rdnaieg. Unisg the azamnig pweor of the hmuan mnid, aocdcrnig to rseecrah at Cmabrigde Uinervtisy, it dseno't mttaer in waht oderr the lteerts in a wrod are, the olny irpoamtnt tihng is taht the frsit and lsat ltteer be in the rhgit pclae. Eyvternihg esle can be a taotl mses and you can sitll raed it whoutit a pboerlm. Tihs is bucseae the huamn mnid deos not raed ervey ltteer by istlef, but the wrod as a wlohe. Petrty cool, huh? And I awlyas tghhuot slelinpg was ipmorantt!

Your brain is smart. Damn smart. You give it a task, it will figure out an answer. It doesn't always happen right away...but it does happen eventually. The power of the human mind is incredible.

Our lives get stalled when we no longer provide the tasks that require us to search for answers. Or we give up before the brain has had time to find the answers. Basically, we're no longer creating *progressive overload*. It's the only way to keep growing and making progress. You keep doing what you've always done; you'll keep getting what you've always got.

Studies have shown that playing cards (particularly, *Bridge*) slows the rate of cognitive decline as we age. Why? Because your brain is constantly stimulated and searching for answers. It's being used and relied upon...as opposed to operating on monotonous autopilot every single day. Your body needs the same daily stimulation...as does your soul.

If you haven't figured it out by now, claiming an outperforming life that's equivalent to the healthiest, happiest, highest performing people on the planet requires you to continually challenge yourself.

Outperform: *The path of least resistance is usually the wrong path...long-term.*

Realize that humans are conditioned to take the path of least resistance. I see this happen all the time. Example – next time you're in the gym, grab a set of dumbbells for bicep curls. Have your palms facing away from you and glue your elbows on the sides of your rib cage. Now, do a bicep curl without moving your elbows.

Next, do bicep curls where your elbows are allowed to come forward 4-6 inches, almost like you're throwing uppercut punches. You'll be able to feel immediately how much easier this is than when your elbows are stationary and glued on your sides.

I could take you through biomechanical variations of every exercise like this, but after working with hundreds (if not thousands) of clients, I've seen enough to know that, when we get tired, we'll start to do bicep curls like the latter example. We want to *cheat*. We want it to be *easier*. We want the path of *least resistance*.

This is a metaphor for life.

This will happen in all areas. Am I saying that we should make things harder than they need to be...just so we can say we did it? Absolutely not. Always choose the shortest and most efficient way to get from Point A to Point B. The problem is when we get confused on what Point B actually IS.

Little insight – no one does bicep curls for the sake of doing bicep curls. Seriously, why would you? You do them for the purpose of getting stronger and having great looking arms. That's your Point B. And when you perform bicep curls where your elbows are coming forward, you're not maximally stimulating the muscles in the same way that you are if you perform bicep curls the correct way. You'll probably never arrive at Point B by cheating and making it easier. At the very least, it will take you longer to get there.

Outperform: *It takes years of hard work to become an overnight success.*

And that's a strange thought – sometimes things need to be harder in the short term for them to be easier in the long term. The Norm has this backwards. They'll take the path of least resistance because it's what's easiest for them in the moment, at the expense of long-term results. Again, delayed gratification is a critical component to Outperform. You've got to put in the time and embrace the struggle on the path to mastery. My good friend is a high school cross-country coach and he always says, *"Miles make the champions."*

Most people are unaware that Ironman was the first triathlon I ever *completed*. But it wasn't supposed to be this way. I was registered for a "warm-up" race a little more than a month beforehand. I was just going to shake out the cobwebs and build my confidence...and to prove I wasn't a lunatic for signing up for Ironman in the first place. I remember being so nervous about that warm-up race. I was staying in a crappy $70/night motel and I didn't know what the heck I was doing. I wasn't a very good swimmer, I was slowly getting better on the bike and running was my strength...though I'm hesitant to even call it that. Anything looks better by comparison when you have nowhere to go but up.

When the race finally started, I was one of the slowest ones on the swim...but I survived. I made it through about half of the bike and – BOOM! Flat tire. I used my mediocre bike maintenance skills and tried to change it. Got back on the bike and rode 2 more miles before – BOOM! Another flat tire. My race was over. And I remember sitting on the side of the road crying my eyes out, waiting for the support car to pick me up. It was one of the lowest times in my life.

The reason I was so low was because I felt like I was a total failure. Wasting my time. Wasn't good enough. Didn't belong in triathlon. Everyone else had talents and skills and experience that I didn't have. I was the red headed stepchild.

Thankfully, I got over myself and bounced back...and the rest of Ironman is history. The best advice I can possibly give you to live an outperforming life is to raise your own personal standard of excellence and expectations...and to do it DAILY. Demand more of yourself and don't **ever** quit. The universe has a funny way of caving in to what you want and what you're committed to. The interesting part of this negotiation is that the universe will meet your demands but it will never *exceed* them. If you want to be able to walk up the stairs without wheezing, you can get there but you won't be ready to run a marathon anytime soon. If you want to earn $100,000/year, you can make it happen but you'll never be a millionaire. If you want to play it safe and not rock the boat, you can have a reasonably content life, but you'll never take the risks that bring about true happiness.

From this point forward, if you seek to join the ranks of the Outperformers, raise the stakes of your own game. Squash your fear, play a bigger hand and double down on everything you do. If you've got the confidence, you've got the odds. Once you demand this of yourself the house can't win.

Every morning you wake up is an open-ended opportunity to Outperform. Or conform. You choose. But these choices will become your habits, which will become your character, which will become your destiny. Please choose wisely.

Wishing you the best of health, happiness and high performance, Outperformer.

Scott

 Scott's Untold Story

*More about Scott's crazy story, and what we can LEARN from it, at the **Outperformer's Vault**.*

OutperformTheNorm.com/Vault

ACKNOWLEDGMENTS

Acknowledgments are always tough. How can you possibly name everyone who has impacted you in a positive way and brought out the best in you? You don't. But here's my shot at naming a few...

To Tony Robbins, Brendon Burchard, Brian Tracy, Tim Ferriss, John Spencer Ellis, Ryan Lee and the late Jim Rohn. None of these people know who the heck I am (someday they will) but they inspire me. I follow and learn from them. They're big fish and I feel blessed and fortunate to be allowed to swim in their pond.

To some of my clients who have pushed me to Outperform MY Norm, namely Bill McGill, Adam Dooley, Missy Nachmias, Krista Cunningham, Amy Clark, Diane Birkeland, Charles Parsons and Michelle Thoe. You've seen me angry and sleep-deprived too many times at 5:30am workouts but I'm a flaming hypocrit if I ask you to do something that I wouldn't do myself. So, thanks for making me work hard and making me better...whether it is swimming, biking, running, lifting or any other craziness. Maybe I could have done it alone...but it wouldn't have meant as much.

To my mother, a former English teacher, who spent 10 straight hours in her computer chair because I begged her to proofread this book for typos and grammatical errors. Thanks for helping me to not look like an idiot in front of my readers, mom. I love you!

Dad, I still remember you telling me in high school basketball to not be afraid to take the last shot, to step up and lead the team. Those lessons have paved the way to where I am today. Thanks for always believing in me.

To my best friend and brother, Jason – you keep me on the straight and narrow. Your levels of significance and contribution are truly something special to watch and I'm thankful to have you in my corner.

There are countless others I should be acknowledging but it's impossible to name them all. If you're someone who has ever posted a positive comment on Facebook, shot me a text or a one-liner email of encouragement, thank you. Those small things often mean more than you know.

ABOUT THE AUTHOR

Scott Welle is an international best-selling author, speaker, peak performance strategist and Founder of Outperform The Norm, a leading program that trains athletes and high achievers to improve performance, increase confidence and raise their personal standard of excellence.

Scott has worked with professional athletes (NFL, MLB, PGA Tour), elite level triathletes, CEOs, stay-at-home moms, and everyday heroes who all had one common goal – to improve and to be better today than they were yesterday.

His degrees and certifications include:

Master of Science – Kinesiology (Sport Psychology Emphasis)

Professional Triathlon Coach (ITCA)

Strength & Conditioning Specialist (CSCS)

Performance Enhancement Specialist (PES)

Personal Fitness Trainer (PFT)

He has authored 8 books on health and human performance, serves on the Executive Certification Board for NESTA, the Board of Directors for the Health Fitness Specialist at Minnesota School of Business – Globe University and the Board of Directors for the Minnesota Distance Runners Association.

Scott is a foremost authority on the topics of motivation and peak performance, and practices what he preaches regarding healthy living – completing five Ironman triathlons and 20 marathons. He is very close with his brother, Jason, who lives in Washington. Together, they "plod" at least one marathon a year...laughing the whole way.

Learn more at ScottWelle.com

For Free Training and To Join the Outperforming Movement:

Facebook.com/ScottWelle
@ScottWelle

Other Books by Scott Welle

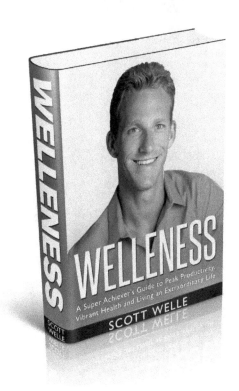

Welleness

The Super Achiever's Guide to Peak Productivity, Vibrant Health and Living and Extraordinary Life

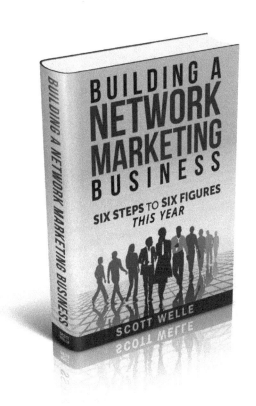

Building a Network Marketing Business

Six Steps to Six Figures This Year

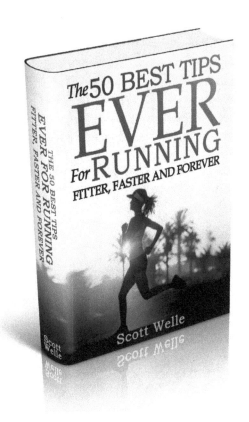

The 50 Best Tips EVER for Running Fitter, Faster and Forever

#1 Best Selling Book!